Metropolitan
PHILIP
His Life and His Dreams

Metropolitan PHILIP

His Life and His Dreams

The Authorized Biography of
His Eminence, Metropolitan PHILIP Saliba
Primate
The Antiochian Orthodox Christian Archdiocese
of North America

Peter E. Gillquist

THOMAS NELSON PUBLISHERS
NASHVILLE

Published in Nashville, Tennessee, by Thomas Nelson, Inc., and distributed in Canada by Lawson Falle, Ltd., Cambridge, Ontario.

Scripture quotations are from the NEW KING JAMES VERSION of the Bible. Copyright © 1979, 1980, 1982, Thomas Nelson, Inc., Publishers.

Library of Congress Cataloging-in-Publication Data

Gillquist, Peter E., 1931–
    Metropolitan Philip : his life and his dreams : the authorized
biography of His Eminence, Metropolitan Philip Saliba, Primate, the
Antiochian Orthodox Christian Archdiocese of North America / by
Peter E. Gillquist.
        p.   cm.
    ISBN 0-8407-7588-1
    1. Saliba, Philip, 1931–   . 2. Antiochian Orthodox Christian
Archdiocese of North America—Bishops—Biography.   3. Orthodox
Eastern Church—Bishops—Biography.   I. Title.
BX738.A759S354   1991
281.9′092—dc20
    [B]   91–13857
                                                                CIP

Printed in the United States of America

1 2 3 4 5 6 7 — 96 95 94 93 92 91

Written to honor
His Eminence, Metropolitan PHILIP,
on the occasion of his
Twenty-fifth Anniversary as Primate of
The Antiochian Orthodox Christian
Archdiocese of North America
1966–1991

CONTENTS

PREFACE

At the outset of this book, two things must be said. First, for those not as familiar with her as they would like to be, let me briefly introduce the Orthodox Christian Church. Secondly, I wish to introduce to you His Eminence, Metropolitan PHILIP Saliba, whose story herein told is intimately related to the understanding of this Church.

THE ORTHODOX CHURCH

From the apostolic age of the Church, we learn directly from the New Testament that the people of God were usually identified geographically. The epistles of St. Paul, for example, were addressed specifically "to the Saints who are in Ephesus" or "to the Church of God which is at Corinth." As we learn in the Pastoral Epistles, soon a bishop would be sent to abide and reside in such cities.

As the gospel spread throughout the ancient

world, and as the Church grew numerically, this same tradition of designating the Church geographically was retained. Thus, one sees developing the Church of Greece, the Church of Antioch, the Church of Crete.

This pattern, which followed a socio-political model, was set by the middle of the fourth century when five patriarchal centers emerged, designated by name after the major metropolitan areas in the world. The patriarchs, or "arch-fathers" who oversaw these city-centers, were the bishops who pastored other bishops in the regions within their authority. These patriarchal centers were, in the order of their existence, Jerusalem, Antioch, Rome, Alexandria, and Constantinople. All five patriarchs enjoyed full communion with each other, and Rome was seen among them as "first among equals."

In the latter part of the first millennium, however, Rome introduced two changes—innovations to which the other four patriarchs and their clergy and laity could not agree. The first of these alterations alleged that the patriarch of Rome (or *pope,* the intimate word for "Father") was not simply the first in honor as had been confessed by all, but rather the universal patriarch, head over the Church throughout the world. The second change had to do with a late addition to the Nicene Creed which changed how the Holy Trinity was understood.

Both of these changes were adopted unilaterally by Rome, and the other patriarchs rejected them on the grounds they were not rooted in the apostolic faith: they were taught neither in the Scriptures nor by the early Church fathers.

The year A.D. 1054 is usually designated as the year in which the Church became tragically divided over these two issues. The four eastern patriarchs continued on, holding the traditional apostolic understanding of the faith, and became known as the Orthodox Church. The Roman patriarch assumed primacy in the west over the Roman Catholic Church.

Within the Orthodox or Eastern Church the national titles of the various jurisdictions continued to be used. To this day for example, one notes the existence of the Antiochian Orthodox Church, the Greek Orthodox, the Russian Orthodox, the Romanian Orthodox and so forth. While the titles designate a specific country, it is imperative to see that the doctrine, worship, and government of the Churches is the very same. And they are all in communion with each other.

The late nineteenth century sets the context for this book. At that time a large influx of Orthodox Christian immigrants came to North America. When they arrived, they, for the most part, retained their national identities. Thus at the close of the twentieth century there are still present on the continent the various jurisdictions of Orthodoxy. Their faith is the same, their liturgies the same (though the language often is not) and their form of polity is the same. But, still, Orthodox Christianity is seen by most observers as being Greek or Russian, Serbian or Bulgarian.

With this brief history in view, the reader will better understand the references in this book to the various national identities within the one Orthodox Church. And this same history must be known if we are to understand the life story of our primate, Metropolitan PHILIP.

THE METROPOLITAN

This authorized biography of His Eminence, Metropolitan PHILIP Saliba, is written by Peter E. Gillquist to mark the 25th anniversary of Philip's episcopal leadership of the Antiochian Orthodox Christian Archdiocese of North America.

His life is a matrix of one fulfilled dream following another, and is wonderfully recorded in this work. This has been a story begging to be told. For the life of Philip Saliba serves as an icon and an inspiration for all who seek to follow Christ, and for those who share his vision of bringing North America to the fullness of the Apostolic Christian faith as it is lived and protected in the Orthodox Church.

We meet this man in his childhood years in a small town outside Beirut, Lebanon, and follow his growth in Christ during school and seminary years. We go with him as a deacon in Damascus, as a student to London, Boston, Detroit and New York, as a priest in Cleveland and as Archbishop to all North America. His dreams and visions, his setbacks and successes are marvelously unveiled, to the extent that the reader will count him as an intimate friend by the book's end.

Having known Philip Saliba all my adult life, and being the first person to enter the holy priesthood by his hand, I commend to you this moving and compelling story.

Father Joseph Allen,
Vicar General,
Antiochian Orthodox
  Christian Archdiocese
  of North America

ACKNOWLEDGMENTS

I wish to recognize and extend sincere personal thanks to a number of people who made possible the writing of this biography.

His Eminence, Metropolitan PHILIP, granted four full days of interviews and two additional day-long sessions for careful review of the material. Further historical material was discovered in conversations with Archpriest Paul Romley, Archdeacon Hans El Hayek, Ted Mackoul, Nassif Saliba, and Ernest Saykaly.

Kathy Meyer opened the archives of the archdiocese, making available virtually all the published records and photographs. At every stage, Shirley Dillon entered the manuscript into the word processor.

An editorial committee consisting of His Grace, Bishop ANTOUN, and Archpriests Joseph Allen and George S. Corey supplied crucial background data through interviews, and then reviewed the final manuscript for accuracy and detail. The Archpriest Jack N. Sparks read the original draft,

strengthening sentence structure and grammar.
To all these people, my sincere thanks.

Father Peter E. Gillquist
Santa Barbara, California

And He
found Philip
and said
to him,
"Follow Me."

JOHN 1:43

MILES

0   25   50   75

Graphic by Luke Dingman

CHRONOLOGY

of the Life of

Metropolitan PHILIP Saliba

1931, June 10	Birth, Abou Mizan, Lebanon.
1936, September	Begins education at Shouier Elementary School.
1945, September	Enters Balamand Orthodox Seminary near Tripoli, Lebanon, at age fourteen.
1948, September	Enrolls at Orthodox Secondary School, Homs, Syria, graduating in 1949.
1949, August 6	Ordained deacon at age nineteen.
1949, September	Assigned as secretary to Patriarch Alexander III in Damascus; enrolls at Assiyeh College, graduating in 1951.
1952, September	Appointed dean of students and lecturer in Arabic languages and literature, Balamand Seminary.
1953, September	Enrolls at Kelham Theological School, Nottinghamshire, England.
1954, September	Enrolls at University of London, London, England.
1956, January	Arrives in the United States, enrolls at Holy Cross Greek

	Orthodox Seminary, Boston (Brookline), Massachusetts.
1956, Fall	Assigned as deacon at St. George Church, Detroit, Michigan, and begins studies at Wayne State University.
1959, January	Graduates, Wayne State University, B.A. in history.
1959, March 1	Ordained to the Orthodox Priesthood by Metropolitan Antony Bashir in Cleveland, Ohio, and assigned as pastor of St. George Church, Cleveland.
1964, September	Enters St. Vladimir's Orthodox Seminary, Crestwood (NYC), New York, graduating with M. Div. in June 1965.
1966, March 16	Nominated Archbishop of New York to succeed Metropolitan Antony Bashir.
1966, June	Elevated to Archimandrite by Metropolitan Ilyas Kurban, in Louisville, Kentucky.
1966, August 5	Elected Archbishop of New York and all North America by the Holy Synod of Antioch.
1966, August 14	Consecrated to the episcopacy by Patriarch Theodosius VI, St. Elias Monastery in Lebanon.
1966, October 13	Enthroned as Metropolitan of North America at the Cathedral of St. Nicholas, Brooklyn, New York.
1968, January	Suffers heart attack in Washington, D.C.

1971, December	Purchase of archdiocesan residence and headquarters, Englewood, New Jersey.
1972, September	Heart bypass surgery, Miami, Florida, is successful.
1973, July	Founds Antiochian Orthodox Christian Women of North America (AOCWNA).
1975, June 24	With Archbishop Michael, effects Antiochian jurisdictional unity in North America, ratified by the Holy Synod of Antioch, August 19, 1975.
1975, July	Founds the Order of St. Ignatius of Antioch. Thirty-four charter members have grown to over one thousand by 1991.
1977, Summer	Patriarch Elias IV comes to North America—the first visit ever of the Patriarch of Antioch to this continent.
1978, March 31	Purchase of Antiochian Village, Ligonier, Pennsylvania.
1981, May	Honorary Doctor of Divinity degree, St. Vladimir's Seminary, Crestwood, New York, where he serves as vice president of the board of trustees.
1985, Summer	Patriarch Ignatius IV visits North America; dedication of Phase I of the Heritage and Learning Center.
1986, May 5	Awarded Doctor of Humane Letters degree, Wayne State University, Detroit, Michigan.

1986, July 1	Receives the cherished "Liberty Award" from Mayor Ed Koch in New York City.
1987, February 8	Begins chrismations and ordinations of the Evangelical Orthodox faithful at St. Michael's Church, Van Nuys, California.
1987, September 11	Meets with Pope John Paul II in Columbia, South Carolina.
1987, December 14	Meets with Vice President George Bush in New York City.
1988, Spring	Tenth Anniversary of Antiochian Village.
1989, Fall	Construction begins on Phase II of the Heritage and Learning Center.
1990, June	Dedication of Phase II, Heritage and Learning Center, Antiochian Village, Ligonier, Pennsylvania.
1991, August 14	Twenty-fifth anniversary of the consecration of Metropolitan Philip Saliba to the Holy Orthodox episcopacy.

1

An Overview: The Church at Antioch

Then Barnabas departed for Tarsus to seek Saul. And when he had found him, he brought him to Antioch. So it was that for a whole year they assembled with the church and taught a great many people. And the disciples were first called Christians in Antioch.

Acts 11:25–26

L ook! shouted the youthful deacon as he stood gazing heavenward, surrounded by his vicious accusers. "I see the heavens opened and the Son of Man standing at the right hand of God!"

His enemies could bear to hear no more.

Stephen had been seized and brought to the council of the high priest in Jerusalem not a half hour earlier. The charge leveled at him was blasphemy: his claim that Jesus of Nazareth would change the customs Moses had delivered to Israel.

Stephen did not deny it. In fact, at the request of the high priest to answer the charge, Stephen had already rehearsed before them just a few moments earlier the entire history of the chosen people of God, starting with Abraham in Mesopotamia. He concluded his defense by showing that Jesus Christ was their promised Messiah, the very Prophet whom Moses had foretold. It was they, Stephen's listeners, whom he in turn charged with betraying this Just One and prejudicially murdering Him.

The members of the council were furious. Some shouted out vehement countercharges; others covered their ears so they could hear no more of Stephen's witness. Together they seized him and dragged him outside the city walls of Jerusalem to stone him.

Watching carefully was a brilliant and influential member of the Sanhedrin, Saul, a man no more than thirty years of age. He had an eerie smile of satisfaction on his face as the stoning began. Ever since Saul had first learned of Jesus, he had done everything possible to silence the claims of His followers. It was apparent to all who witnessed the execution of Stephen: Saul was ultimately behind the scheme.

Gasping for breath and near death in the barrage of flying stones, Stephen summoned the inner strength to whisper in prayer, "Lord Jesus, receive my spirit." He knelt and drew what would be his final breath, crying out at the top of his voice, "Lord, do not charge them with this sin!"

He slumped to the ground, dead.

THE DISPERSION

Stephen's death was the first among what would become countless others. For that very day the falling asleep of the protomartyr launched a persecution throughout Jerusalem of those who were identified with this assembly, this Church which they said Jesus had begun. Except for the apostles, numbers of new believers left the city and scattered throughout the towns and villages of Judea and on to neighboring Samaria.

Saul noted keenly this movement of the people. He saw to it that those of the Church who did not leave Jerusalem were either forced from their homes or imprisoned, both men and women.

Those who left Jerusalem, however, were in no way silenced. Everywhere they went they preached the Word of God, telling those they met about Jesus Christ. Miracles accompanied their preaching, and for the first time people who were not Jews heard about the Messiah and believed in Him.

THE GOSPEL COMES TO ANTIOCH

Some who were exiled went north along the coast of the Great Sea as far as the province of Phoenicia, and then across to the island of Cyprus. Together with a group of Cypriots, a number of men traveled up to Syria and arrived in Antioch, a city known throughout that expansive region as the "Queen of the East." Antioch was a melting pot of people—Arabs, Jews, Greeks, Romans—the capital of Syria. She was recognized in the ancient world as the bridge city between East and West.

When the people of Antioch were confronted by these newcomers with the proclamation of Jesus Christ, a great number of them believed and turned to the Lord. News of the conversion of these Antiochians reached the Church back in Jerusalem. The apostles there, in turn, sent Barnabas to Antioch to establish these new believers in the faith. The year was A.D. 38.

Meanwhile something else had taken place, something miraculous. As the persecution of the disciples in Jerusalem continued, the instigator of the opposition to the Church himself experienced an abrupt and dramatic conversion to Christ. It happened as he was on a journey from Jerusalem to Damascus. Intending to inflict new harm upon the Church, that energetic enemy of the faith, Saul of Tarsus, was personally confronted by the Son of God in a vision! The ascended Lord, surrounded by the uncreated light of heaven itself, stopped him short: "Saul, Saul," He demanded, "why are you persecuting Me?"

Saul, struck instantly to the ground by this dazzling blaze of glory, was overcome by the light—a light so bright and real it not only struck Saul blind, but was seen by his companions as well.

"Go to Damascus," Jesus told him. "There you will be told all things which are appointed for you to do."

In Damascus, Saul met the prophet Ananias, who, after speaking with him, laid hands on him that he might receive the gift of the Holy Spirit. The newly baptized Saul would become

Paul, the great apostle, the messenger to the Gentiles, the one who would one day suffer and die himself for the Christ who had saved him.

In Antioch, the new Church continued to prosper as a community and to grow. With Barnabas in their midst to encourage them, a great number of new people were brought to Christ and to His Church. Before long Barnabas needed help. Where could he turn for assistance? *What about Saul?* he thought as he remembered the zealous new convert who was now back in his hometown of Tarsus, some eighty miles to the west. Barnabas went there himself and brought Saul back to Antioch as his co-worker. Together, these two gifted apostles of Christ taught the Antiochian community the Word of God for a full year. During this time the followers of the Lord Jesus in Antioch were first called Christians.

In the early forties, after the year of instruction in Antioch by Paul and Barnabas was complete, the two men journeyed to Jerusalem and remained there for a time. Then it was back home to Antioch.

Presumably it was on a Sunday morning, perhaps in the year 45. The Antiochian Christians were together in the liturgy of the Lord and fasting, when the Holy Spirit spoke to them saying, "Separate to Me Barnabas and Saul for the work to which I have called them." From the Church at Antioch would go forth perhaps the most impor-

tant mission team the Christian Church has ever
known. The first of their apostolic journeys took
place from A.D. 46 to 48.

Antioch had been the first major city outside of Jerusalem to hear the gospel of Christ. But
now the Word of God spread to other important
centers of the world as well, including Ephesus,
Corinth, and Rome. In the decade of the fifties, ancient tradition reveals that the apostle Peter became
the first bishop of Antioch, and in the early sixties
he moved on to become bishop of Rome. He was
martyred there, together with Paul, in A.D. 65. Because of the influence of these godly apostles, the
Church of Antioch has often been called the
Church of St. Peter and St. Paul.

Later in the sixties—A.D. 67 is the often accepted date—another apostolic leader arose in the
Queen City and became the bishop there, the venerable Ignatius of Antioch. Ignatius is an important leader in the early Church, for he spanned the
years between the twelve apostles and the early
fathers of the Church.

Ignatius served as bishop or patriarch of
Antioch from A.D. 67 to 107, when he was martyred in Rome. In existence to this day are the seven
letters he wrote shortly before his death to encourage the bishops of the neighboring Churches in the
surrounding cities. These letters, included in the
volume *The Apostolic Fathers,* secure in history
the first-century presence of bishops throughout

the Church, surrounded by their priests and their deacons.

ANTIOCH IN CHURCH HISTORY

Early in the history of the Church at Antioch a school was begun to teach the "memoirs of the apostles," the Holy Scriptures, to Christians from the city and the surrounding area who came for instruction. From this school would come many of the most noted saints and martyrs of the ancient Church.

In the summer of A.D. 325, the first great ecumenical council of the Church was held in the city of Nicaea to deal with the eternality of the person of the Son of God. Interestingly, the first portion of the creed to emerge from this council was written in Antioch. Earlier that year, the obnoxious activity of the Arians (those who held that there was a time when the Son of God did not exist) had brought about the calling together of a regional council at Antioch. The participants studied a letter written by Alexander, the pious bishop of Alexandria, underscoring the divinity of Jesus Christ and condemning the beliefs of those who taught that the Son of God was a creature, whose existence began at a point in time. The document that came out of this Antiochian council was expanded later that same year in the Council of Nicaea to become what we know as the original Nicene Creed.

Antioch—together with Rome, Alexandria, Jerusalem, and Constantinople—was recognized throughout the world as one of the five great patriarchal centers of Christendom. The Antiochian school of biblical exegesis continued to grow in importance. In contrast to the school of Alexandria, which favored a somewhat allegorical handling of the Scriptures, Antioch was known for its commitment to a more literal interpretation of the Bible and an aggressive preaching and teaching of the gospel of Christ. In this connection, the most famous son of the Church at Antioch was St. John Chrysostom.

John's birth is set at approximately 344 in Antioch. He was raised in a Christian home by a widowed mother. He cared for her until her death in 373, and then for four years he was a hermit monk in the mountains just outside the city. He returned to Antioch in 381 and was ordained deacon by Patriarch Meletius. John became a priest five years later by the hands of Patriarch Flavian and was given the specific task of preaching at the Orthodox cathedral in Antioch.

In this Church at Antioch over the next decade John delivered the sermons that today make up his various commentaries on the New Testament Gospels and Epistles. Against his will, John was consecrated Patriarch of Constantinople in 398. He served a short term of distinction, was exiled in 403, and died four years later. In the sixth century, as Christian people read and were edified by his writings, John was affectionately nicknamed Chrysostomos, meaning "golden mouthed."

Antioch was the heart of vital Christianity in the Middle East. She produced a host of inspired teachers and preachers of Orthodox Christianity. But present as well was a jagged line of detractors and heretics who stood against true faith and the doctrine of the apostles.

As Chrysostom closed his days as Patriarch of Constantinople, the monastery at Antioch brought forth another gifted preacher, Nestorious, who would go on to be head of the entire Eastern Church. But unlike his predecessor, John Chrysostom, Nestorious would stop short of upholding the Orthodox Christian faith. For he would heretically separate Christ into two persons—one divine and one human—opposing the apostolic understanding of Christ as one divine Person in two natures. Nestorious, ultimately removed from the See of Constantinople, fostered one of the tragic, historic schisms from true Christianity.

But in the faithful tradition of John Chrysostom another bright light of the Antiochian See would emerge in the seventh century, St. John of Damascus. Later known as a doctor of the Church, this brilliant scholar and theologian was born in Damascus in about 675 to a wealthy Christian family. For a time, as a young adult, he held his father's previous post as the chief representative of the Christian community to the head of state, the caliph. But so as not to compromise his loyalty to the Church of Christ, John resigned that post and entered a Christian monastery near Jerusalem in 716. There he was ordained to the priesthood.

John of Damascus is known for his outstanding theological writing and is even better remembered as the staunch defender of Christian imagery prior to the famed Seventh Ecumenical Council. His theological precision and biblical exegesis is generally credited for preserving the use of Christian icons in the homes of the faithful and in the churches.

THE CHURCH OF ANTIOCH TODAY

Damascus, on the "street called straight" where the apostle Paul was sent after his conversion to Christ, the present-day patriarch of Antioch now dwells, as he has since the fifteenth century when the Turks overran the city of Antioch. Ignatius IV, Patriarch of Antioch since 1979, oversees Orthodox faithful in the Middle East and abroad. He is represented in America by the Antiochian Orthodox Christian Archdiocese of North America, headquartered in suburban New York City.

The Antiochian Orthodox Church has been present in the new world of North America since the mid 1800s. True to its history of preaching, teaching, and evangelism under great Christian saints like Paul the apostle, John Chrysostom, and John of Damascus, today's Christians of Antioch carry with them the same spirit of biblical fidelity, vision, and dedication. In North America, Bishop of Antioch Raphael Hawaweeny first used the English language in worship in the early 1900s.

To this day, the Church of Antioch marches at the front of the column of Orthodox progress in seeking to bring America face to face with the changeless treasure of New Testament Christianity. Guiding the Antiochian Archdiocese in North America since 1966 is the remarkable Metropolitan Philip Saliba. It is his gripping life story which is presented in the pages that follow.

2

Road to Damascus

Arise and go into the city,
and you will be told what
you must do.

Acts 9:6

The tiny village of Abou Mizan is hidden in the verdant hills of Lebanon fifteen miles to the east of Beirut. To this day it is still a small, humble, rural community composed of some thirty or forty country homes, set peacefully amid cultivated fields and vineyards in the shadow of beautiful Mount Sanneen.

Things have changed little from the 1920s and 1930s, the years that Elias Saliba and his young bride, Saleema, bought some land, built their home, and began to raise their children. By 1930 the family had grown to five. Nassif, the eldest son, was eight, followed by a second son, Shaheed, six, and a two-year-old daughter, Nazera.

AN ANNOUNCEMENT

As the first chill of autumn touched the air that year, Saleema realized a fourth child was to join the family. She pulled Elias aside as he returned from work one evening in November. Her dark eyes sparkled, and she smiled warmly as she touched his arm. "There will be a new baby in early June," she whispered in his ear.

Elias was a farmer and a builder. He had begun both trades as a young man working for his father and had gradually saved enough money to buy the land. He began to cultivate this land, together with some adjacent acreage owned by the nearby Orthodox Monastery of St. Elias. Many of the men in Abou Mizan worked under the same arrangement, farming their own land and that owned by the monastery.

Saleema's work was in her home. She especially loved baking bread and cooking the meals for her growing family. She also kept silkworms; producing silk was the home trade of many women in rural Lebanon. As in many homes, the downstairs of the Saliba house was one large room to facilitate the spinning and weaving of silk.

In the spring Saleema ordinarily helped her husband with the planting, but not this spring. For with the baby soon to come, Nassif assumed more of her tasks, and Shaheed was learning to be helpful, too. By the middle of May, Saleema limited herself to preparing meals, washing the clothes, and caring for her children.

On a warm and bright Wednesday, June 10, 1931, she gave birth to Philip.

But his given name was not Philip. It was Abdallah, "the servant of God" in Arabic. Later, at his ordination to the diaconate, he would be

named after Philip the apostle of Christ. His grandfather was Abdallah, and in Arabic tradition one of
the grandsons—often the first—takes his paternal
grandfather's name.

Elias saved the name for his third son on
purpose.

"He always felt one of us four boys would be
a priest," Nassif recalled years later. "That is why, I
believe, our father named him Abdallah. He anticipated him to be that priest who would serve the
Lord."

Next door lived another Saliba household.
Elias' brother, Naif, and his family resided there.
Before long, the two brothers would have virtually
identical families, four boys and a girl. The cousins
became inseparable. Especially and mischievously
close knit were the eight boys, to the point of trying
the patience of their sisters and their mothers.

Life together, of course, heightens both joy
and sorrow. With no sign or warning, Naif died
suddenly, not long after the birth of his fifth child.
His passing was a painful shock, for he was still
very young. Without hesitation Elias took full re-
sponsibility for both families. With Elias and Saleema's fourth son, Najib, having been born in
1933, Philip had the sense of being raised in a family of ten children, eight boys and two girls.

The children all stood in stunned awe of
Elias. When he was away at work during the day,
the eight boys turned the two houses upside down;
Saleema and her sister-in-law were staggered by the

impossible assignment of keeping full order. But as soon as Elias returned home each evening, the boys became angelic—or at least pseudo-angelic.

EARLY YEARS

Philip's earliest memories have to do with those wonderful evenings at home. "All of us, our family and our cousins, loved to sing. So we formed a little choir. During Advent, right before Christmas, we sang that hymn known so well to all Orthodox Christians the world over: 'Christ Is Born! Glorify Him!' Perhaps this is one of the reasons I grew to love the Church so much. As a child I was absolutely taken with the singing of the hymns."

Each year the whole family looked forward to Christmas with great expectation. On Christmas Eve the drama of anticipation heightened.

The abbot at the Monastery of St. Elias was always sure to send a priest into the village of Abou Mizan every Christmas to serve the three-hour liturgy of Christ's birth for all the faithful. Arriving late on Christmas Eve, he rang the bell in the church at three o'clock on Christmas morning, and it echoed throughout the valley. Everybody in the village awakened to the melody.

There were few roads in the mountains around the village. The people made their way by foot across the hillsides, on the paths made by their forebears, walking carefully through the predawn darkness to join the entire village at the tiny candle-lit church.

Always careful to keep the fast before Holy Communion, the people ate nothing at all before the service. But after worship on Christmas morning they feasted to celebrate the Birth of Christ, the Incarnation of the Son of God. Families gathered in their homes for a huge breakfast with relatives and friends, and afterward people went from house to house in the village visiting for hours with each other.

But it wasn't Christmas alone that formed the matrix of early memories for young Philip.

"Our life in the village, as I remember from my childhood, centered around the Church—the holidays—Christmas, Easter, the Feast of St. George who was the patron saint of our little church, and the Feast of the Dormition on August 15. The whole village turned out together. You have to remember, there were no radios or TVs or CDs. Life was utterly simple. The life of the village was the Church."

As a powerful preacher and communicator today, Philip is hard pressed to remember any of the sermons he heard as a young man from the visiting priest. "But I do recall how we used to go to church on Good Friday and decorate the bier of Christ with flowers and then gather together to sing—all of us, the entire population of the village. We spent the whole day on Good Friday picking flowers from the field and cutting branches of trees to bring to the church. Carrying the branches, singing, decorating—I remember these things so very vividly."

Life at home for the Saliba family was pleasant, intimate, secure—but spartan. Elias and Saleema worked with their hands and loved their family. Material possessions were few. But what they had, they shared. They were respected in the village, friendly to all; their home was always open to the people who lived around them.

The eldest son, Nassif, who to this day lives with his wife, Adma, in Shreen, just two miles from his boyhood home, remembers with clarity the atmosphere of the home in which he, Philip, and the others were raised. "Our mother always admonished us to love one another. If one of us was weak, the stronger would help his brother. He who is affluent should help the poor, starting with his own family. She used the example of holding a bunch of small sticks in your hand. If you take out one stick by itself, you can break it every easily. But if you put all the sticks together, side by side, they will not break.

"Or, she would tell us the story of two brothers. One was married, the other single. Together they planted a field of wheat. When harvest came, they gathered the wheat and bound it together in two shocks—one for the single man and one for the married man. Then both of the brothers rose up to go their separate ways, taking their harvest home.

"The single one thought, 'Well, my brother is married. He has many responsibilities with his wife and family. Let me go to his house while he is asleep, and I will add some of my wheat to his so he will have more for his children.' The single man then went over to his brother's home with an arm-load of wheat.

"Later, the married man said to himself, 'My single brother is going to have a wife and chil-dren in the future, so let me give him a little of my wheat.' And he brought him some by night. Both brothers kept on with this, and for each one the supply of wheat never went down!"

In addition to farming the land surrounding his house, Elias Saliba worked as a builder for a construction company near his home. His excel-lence as a stonecutter came to be well-known in the area. Rather than wait for rough-hewn stones to be brought to the building site, he went directly to the quarry where the stones were being removed from the earth. There he cut the stones and shaped them for the job on which he was working—a special stone for the corner of the building, another for the threshold, one for the lintel, one for above the win-dow. He developed a special talent—and earned a reputation—for carving stones that always seemed to fit when they were brought to the work site. He had a mental image of how the stones should fit, and his skill matched the image.

Closely related to this talent was another, one for which he was even more admired. He had become an expert bridge builder when he went to work for a French construction firm in business in Lebanon and throughout the Mediterranean area. Besides constructing bridges, the company built airports, highways, and hotels. Elias held this job while the children were still very young.

Bridges in Lebanon in the mid 1930s were, of course, not erected of steel. They were made of large, carefully hewn stones. Elias used his stone-cutting talent to shape the stones at the quarry and then fit each one into place in the bridge, carved and angled to fit with precision next to the others. The bridges were semicircular, and his work had to be exact. The French firm was very pleased with his work. To this day some of his bridges punctuate the landscape in the hills east of Beirut.

Occasionally, the people living in and around the larger area called Shreen would ask, "Among the Saliba boys, will any grow to be a bridge builder like their father?"

When there was construction to be done, Elias spent long days on the site—cutting, hauling, and fitting his stones together. When there was no work for the company, he thrived on clearing his land, cutting the trees, and planting crops and fruit trees to provide food for his active family.

Nassif remembers, "With Philip and Najib being the youngest, our father loved them so very much. He would try to take a nap when work was done, and rest for the next day. Whenever he went to sleep, one of the boys would lie down beside him on his right, the other on his left.

"As they lay there next to him, Philip waited until his father was in a deep sleep. Then he pinched Najib under the blanket. Najib sat up with a start and screamed, and father woke up and spanked both of them.

"Then, Philip learned a lesson. If, when he pinched Najib and Najib screamed, Philip immediately started to sing the hymn of the Church at Epiphany, this would take away the attention from him. Father assumed he was doing nothing amiss, that Philip was being a good boy."

One evening Elias awoke because of the noise and yelled at Najib, "What are you doing? What is this noise?"

Najib said, "My brother is pinching me."

Elias replied, "No, he is singing!"

"Well, you feel his hand under the blanket, and you will see whether he is chanting the hymn or making trouble!" Najib answered.

Meanwhile, Philip was absolutely undistracted, singing:

> By thy baptism, O Lord in the River
> Jordan,
> Worship to the Trinity has made its
> appearance;
> For the voice of the Lord
> Came forth to Thee with the
> testimony,

Naming Thee beloved Son,
And the Spirit in the likeness of a
dove,
Confirming the truth of the Word.

All in all, life in the home and in the tiny
village was very simple, very focused, very memorable for the young Philip. The two-story house
was alive with activity. Life was lived on the first
floor in the daytime in the large room which served
as kitchen, storeroom, living area, and domestic
silk and textile factory.

In the evening, the boys carried in wood
from outside and loaded and lighted the stove for
heat. The entire family adjourned to the large
room on the second floor to rest for the night.

Then at daybreak, the household—indeed,
the whole village—rose to greet the coming day.
The workers went to the fields, sharing in the labors together. Village people did everything together. If there was a death in the village, everyone
came to the funeral. If a marriage took place, the
villagers all participated in the wedding, for all
were invited. Ancient Christian phrases such as
"One Lord, one faith, one hope" needed little com-
mentary: they seemed simply to interpret themselves.

SCHOOL DAYS

Like his brothers, Philip spent his days either working with his father or studying at the vil-

lage school. He was quiet, pensive, observant. His values took on definition early. This was good; that was bad. He shunned street words and often rebuked the other boys at school for using them. His presence from very early childhood seemed to command respect. He was strikingly handsome, generally taller than others of his age, of strong opinion, and a careful student.

At the village school, a perceptive instructor of the elementary-level children noticed that Philip was gifted with a beautiful voice for both singing and speaking. With good knowledge of Arabic music, he formed a student choir, which included Philip. The youth excelled in languages as well, Arabic at first and later English at another school in a neighboring village. Arabic literature and poetry captivated him from the start.

"Like the village, our school was also very simple, and it was tough," Philip recalls. "Our teachers seemed like tyrants to us. We really didn't like school that much, because if you didn't do your homework you were punished. They made you put one knee on the floor, or stand up facing the wall for hours."

THE PATRIARCHAL VISIT

When Philip was barely fourteen, something very dramatic happened. He remembers it well.

"Our Patriarch, Alexander III, used to come

every summer to St. Elias Monastery because the area was virtually a summer resort. The monastery is just over two miles away from our village. The Patriarch loved the grapes my father grew.

"One Sunday morning in late July, my father woke me early and said 'You know, Patriarch Alexander is at the monastery this morning, and we must visit him and take him some grapes. We will attend the liturgy at the Church of St. Elias.'

"I was very excited. So I went with my father and carried the basket of grapes. We walked from the village up the mountain to the monastery.

"The priest at St. Elias knew us well. He remembered that I had a decent voice, so when he saw us walk into the church and the time came for the reading of the epistle, he asked me to do the reading. Needless to say I was trembling because to read the epistle in the presence of the Patriarch was sobering. But God gave me the courage to read, and I recall I did a good job.

"When the service was over, we went to meet the Patriarch over Arabic coffee and to chat with him. He looked at me and said, 'You have a nice voice,' and I said 'Thank you.'

"Then he looked at my father. 'The Balamand Seminary is going to reopen next year [it was closed during World War II]. I want your son to go to Balamand and become a priest.'

"My father looked at Patriarch Alexander and said, 'Who am I to say no? If it is the will of

God that my son become a priest, then may His will be done.'"

The whole thing started with a basket of grapes!

Elias had not forgotten the reason behind the name he had given his son. Shortly after supper one evening in late summer, Elias called a family conference. "Now that Abdallah has finished his initial schooling, we must decide what is the next step," he said.

"He must go on to school," Nassif, now twenty-three, insisted. "Let us give him support. Shaheed and I will work to help you."

THE YEARS AT BALAMAND

In September of 1945, some twenty to thirty boys, all of them in their teens, enrolled in the first postwar class at Balamand. Philip, at fourteen, was among the oldest of the seminarians.

The dean of the school was the well-loved Bishop Sergios. He was like a father to the young men and cared deeply for them. He was particular about how they slept and where they slept, how they ate and what they ate. His love for Christ and for the students permeated the school, and the fellowship among them all deepened with each passing day.

But there was discipline as well. The wake-up call sounded at five each morning. The cold water in which the boys washed seemed extra chilling because there was no heat in the building.

One of the close friendships Philip established at Balamand was with another seminarian his age, Antoun Khouri, who came from Damascus. Antoun arrived at school in December, two months after classes began. It was Saturday, and the students were preparing their clothes for Sunday worship. Philip was the tallest of the boys at Balamand and seemed to know his way around.

"Where can I go for a shoe shine?" Antoun asked him.

"Go to the bishop," Philip instructed. "We ask him anything we want, and he gives it to us."

The newcomer found the dean's office. "Saidna Sergios," he said, "I would like a shoe shine."

"What makes you think I have one to give?" the Bishop replied, sensing a prank. "Who sent you here?"

"This tall fellow," Antoun answered, describing in detail the student whose name he had not yet learned.

"Oh, Abdallah . . ." The bishop rolled his eyes.

"Is your name Abdallah?" Antoun asked him that night in the dorm room. Philip smiled and nodded yes as he got into bed. "Why did you embarrass me with the bishop by telling me to get from him a shoe shine?" Philip simply smiled again.

The two young men would grow up together and become inseparable in a friendship destined to last a lifetime, seasoned through the years
with both love and laughter.

"What impressed me most about those
years at Balamand," Philip recounts, "was the love
we developed for each other, the strong sense of
oneness, and most importantly the cycle of prayer
which became part of our lives. I learned well the
liturgical structure of the day because of those
three years I spent on that holy hill. The world was
wonderfully far away from us. We loved that little
paradise."

After the five o'clock wake up, the seminarians had half an hour to wash and get dressed.
They studied for an hour, and then went to matins
at six-thirty. Afterwards, breakfast was followed by
morning classes. Instruction included French, music, Arabic, English, and arithmetic.

"I loved the languages. So during arithmetic
I hid my Arabic language book inside my math
book so the teacher could not see it. While he was
explaining the problems, I was reading an Arabic
novel," Philip confesses. "Figures were abstract
things to me. So what if 2 + 2 makes 4. Big deal!
But I always managed to make passing grades in
math, and I pulled down A's in history and literature."

Other courses at Balamand included theology and Church history. Though the instructors
were brilliant, they stayed away from heavy peda-

gogy. The students were young and were in the process of building an educational background from which to understand the highly developed theology that came later. Together they experienced Orthodox Christian worship and learned as much Church history and theology as could be absorbed.

In Lebanon, the national sport is volleyball. The school at Balamand formed and fielded a team, and Philip was its anchor. The seminary overlooks the Mediterranean Sea on the west, and to the east are the beautiful cedars of Lebanon, so walking was a favorite form of exercise as well.

The closest to God Philip ever felt as a young man was at Balamand: "The Patriarch used to come and visit us, and whenever he celebrated the presanctified liturgy during Lent you smelled not only the incense in the Church but the fragrance of the lemon trees outside. John Chrysostom said, 'Lent is the springtime of our souls.' We vividly experienced that renewal as we worshiped together. Spring was the most beautiful time in the mountains. And the music! Patriarch Alexander was a great musician. His voice still rings in my ears. To this day I feel nostalgic when I think of him singing those glorious Lenten hymns."

Each summer Philip returned home to Abou Mizan. He chanted for the village church and spent much of his time at nearby St. Elias Monastery where he had launched his life of service to God that day in 1944 when he and his father brought the basket of grapes to the Patriarch.

THE SCHOOL AT HOMS

After the years at Balamand, Philip became restless, a restlessness that would mark his early years in the ministry. He always wanted to be on the move. After three rewarding years at a level of education that approximates secondary school in the new world, he applied for admission to the head of the Orthodox school at Homs, Archbishop Alexandros Geha. He was accepted and invited to come.

The school at Homs is in Syria, just north of the border of Lebanon. It is on the level of a junior college. When Philip arrived he was invited to move in with Archbishop Alexandros. The hierarch had been educated in Russia, and he kept the fullness of the Russian liturgical cycle to the letter. Every evening the students prayed together at the Church of the Forty Holy Martyrs.

The school at Homs was a public school run by the Church but essentially a secular school that welcomed everybody. As in his days at Balamand, Philip craved literature: "My father used to send me a little money. Other students would buy candy or food. I would save money and buy literary magazines and books."

He liked the biographies best. And fiction—

short fiction. "I don't have patience for long fiction, especially when it comes to Russian novels. Those fictions seem endless."

Next to the lives of the saints, Philip liked the stories of military heroes and reformers of Middle Eastern countries. The era of Arab nationalism was beginning while he was at Homs. The Middle East was emerging from its insecurity of the years after the Second World War. Nationalistic fervor dominated both Lebanon and Syria. A whole new genre of patriotic poetry emerged as well, works that portrayed the Arab-Israeli war of 1947–48, which was fought when he was still at Homs. His horizons, his bounds, and his world were rapidly expanding.

Perhaps the first hint that the young man Philip would become a leader in the Church came in an invitation extended to him in 1949. When he was still nineteen, the same Patriarch Alexander who had found in him potential for the priesthood at age thirteen now, six years later, selected Philip as his personal secretary. The young student from Homs set out on the road to Damascus.

The archimandrite who had served for years as Patriarch Alexander's secretary now wanted to go to Athens to complete his theological study. Where could Alexander turn for help? He telephoned the archbishop at Homs. "You know Philip is my student," he said. "I sent him to Balamand and loaned him to you. I want him back to be my secretary."

Philip had no knowledge of the call until Archbishop Alexandros summoned him to his office the next day. "The Patriarch wants you to go to Damascus because you are one of his handpicked students. You are to be his secretary." The young man sat speechless.

While he in no way felt prepared to be secretary to the Patriarch or to fulfill the awesome demands of that position, he decided, as he would so many times in the years ahead, to put on his cloak of courage and face the challenge with determination. He stood to his feet, thanked the archbishop, and returned to his room.

ON TO DAMASCUS

That summer of 1949, Philip was ordained deacon at the Church of the Transfiguration in Dhour Cheweir near St. Elias Monastery on the Feast of the Transfiguration. Antoun Khouri, still a subdeacon, served as his sponsor. As patriarchal secretary, Philip handled all the correspondence in Arabic. Patriarch Alexander himself wrote the letters to Greek or Russian correspondents.

Philip still desired to continue his education. So in addition to traveling with the Patriarch and overseeing his correspondence, he enrolled as a student at Assiyeh College in Damascus.

At the patriarchate the young deacon was, for the most part, trained on the job. "I learned how to type in Arabic there in the office. I wrote his dictation in long hand, then typed it. To this day, when I need a letter in Arabic, I type it myself."

The years with Patriarch Alexander were formative ones for the energetic, passionate Philip. Of Alexander, he says, "He was one of the most brilliant personalities I have ever met. He was an outstanding musician, a careful scholar. He was fluent in Greek and Russian and even French and Turkish. He also knew some English. I cannot say enough about him."

But there was more. As is so often the case, brilliance was accompanied by a perfectionistic spirit. Philip admits that his own sense of wanting things done right must partly be attributed to the perfectionism of Patriarch Alexander: "The man would not compromise. His services were always done just right."

How right is just right? Deacon Philip was to learn firsthand his first Christmas in Damascus, 1949.

"The biblical account of Christmas is, for me, a joyful story—a beautiful story. I was extremely happy that particular Christmas Day, and the Cathedral of the Holy Dormition in Damascus was packed full with worshipers. All my close friends were there. I was called upon by His Beatitude to read the Gospel."

In the Orthodox Church the Scriptures are read in a set way, according to centuries of Christian tradition. Actually, the Holy Gospel is not read nor sung, but *chanted*.

Metropolitan Philip continues, "With this great joy in my heart, I reached the place in the Christmas Gospel in Matthew 2:1–12 where it says the Magi came and brought gifts of gold, frankincense, and myrrh. These expressions in Arabic are so magnificent and poetical, and I was exuberant. So I departed from the accepted chant and broke out into what sounded like a joyous and melodic Arabic desert song."

"What kind of music is that?" the Patriarch interrupted abruptly as he turned to stare at his deacon from behind the royal doors. "That is not chanting; it is singing!"

Immediately, Philip went back to the prescribed chant.

When the reading of the Gospel is finished, the rubrics call for the deacon to return to the royal doors, present the Gospel Book to the Patriarch for him to venerate and place on the altar. As Philip handed him the Book, the Patriarch warned, "If you ever again sing the Gospel like this, I am going to cut your salary!" In U.S. funds, Philip earned less than a dollar a month.

Today as metropolitan, Philip acknowledges that this now humorous incident was his first memorable lesson in the ministry: While he maintains his standards, a great disciplinarian must never operate in such a way as to create a gap between himself and those who serve him.

A second incident was not so amusing.

"The patriarchal hierarchs never ate with

us, and that pained me because I'm such an idealist. They ate sumptuous food; we were served horrid food. The Patriarch ate by himself or with other bishops, but never with the deacons," Philip recalls.

Philip's response almost put him out of the Church. A group of Philip's friends, students at Assiyeh College, including Antoun Khouri, decided they could take neither the food nor the isolation any longer. When they called a hunger strike, Deacon Philip joined them.

Patriarch Alexander called him in. "What is going on with you?" he demanded.

"I refuse to eat the food you give us because it is so bad," Philip answered boldly.

"But you are my secretary," Alexander assured him. "You belong to me. You can eat my food."

"I don't want to eat your food! Not while my friends are suffering with this second-class fare. I want to eat your food with them."

As the Patriarch struggled to keep his composure, Deacon Philip turned around and walked out. He stopped by his room for his books and headed out of the compound and down the street. He checked into a small hotel a few blocks away.

The next day, a group of influential Orthodox people came to call on him. They urged him to return to the Patriarch and ask forgiveness. He moved out of the hotel and went back with them.

In his office the next day, Alexander told his

understudy, "Look, I am like your father. I may bark at you, but don't take it so seriously and leave."

"These students cannot survive on this food you serve them," Philip persisted. "Please do something about the food."

After three years in Damascus, restlessness again set in. The Patriarch took note of his unsettled spirit and urged his deacon to go to Russia or to Greece for theological study. But Philip had watched those who had studied at the great theological centers of Orthodoxy. They came back proud, looking down on others, and they often became bishops. *That's not for me,* he thought to himself. *They're so untouchable. Bishops should be with their people, interact with their clergy. Why all this isolation?*

Finally, Philip made an appointment with Patriarch Alexander. "I have no interest," he said. "I don't want to go to Greece or study in Russia."

"Then where do you want to go?" the Patriarch demanded.

"I want to go to England."

3

Crisis across the Channel

Jesus said to him, "I am the way, the truth, and the life. No one comes to the Father except through Me."

John 14:6

The Patriarch was not at all pleased. "You mean you want to go to England and learn theology from the Anglicans?" he challenged.

For Philip, a broadened theological education was not at the forefront of his mind. Instead, it was the study of literature, English literature. As for theology, he had received at least a foundational knowledge from the Orthodox instruction at Balamand, Homs, and Assiyeh, plus the three years of hands-on experience at the patriarchate.

Then too, there was the other aspect of his enchantment with England. He had discussed it with no one, but Philip knew his intimates would hear it if they listened between his sentences and words. He wanted to get away.

Predictably, the major obstacle to studying in England was money. How could he afford to go? Patriarch Alexander was not about to offer him a scholarship. In fact, the Patriarch did not offer even a tacit blessing for the young man's plan.

"Okay," Philip reasoned with his superior, "give me permission to return to Balamand to teach Arabic and serve as dean of students." He was buying time.

"All right, if that's what you want. But I am not pleased," the Patriarch said firmly. Philip's long-time friend, Antoun Khouri, took over some of the work Philip had done at the patriarchate.

INSTRUCTOR AND DEAN

In September 1952, Deacon Philip Saliba left Damascus for the Balamand school. His feelings were mixed. England still beckoned, but for now he was fully committed to teaching Arabic literature and to serving as the dean of students. He remembers it as one of the best years of his life. And he was doing something he loved—teaching the Arabic language.

"I established a wonderful relationship with the students," he recalls. "I was, on the one hand, one of them. Yet they respected me as their dean and their teacher. We played volleyball together. We swam together. I wanted to offer them a new reality, a new way of working together, which was contrary to what they had experienced with others in authority—bishops or deans or priests—who were almost always above them."

Again at Balamand, the problem with food emerged. The abbot of the monastery, who was in charge of buying food for the school, bought special food for himself. Even during the fast, students complained they could smell the aroma of fried chicken coming from his quarters. But the students—and the new dean—were stuck with eating the roots of vegetables, stale bread, and starches. It was the same every day. There was neither flavor nor nourishment.

On the day the students decided to go on strike, the dean of students was off campus, on an errand to nearby Tripoli. When Philip returned to campus, he discovered that one of the students had clashed face to face with the abbot because of the food—in front of all the other students. The abbot had slapped him around and spoken crassly to him. But the seminarian was aggressive, a tough guy, and he did not take well to the reprimand nor did he turn the other cheek. Philip returned to a student body up in arms and to an abbot ready to relieve the dean of students of his post.

"The abbot wants to see you," someone shouted to Philip as he returned to the dorm.

"You will have to expel this student," the abbot began bluntly as Philip stepped inside his office.

"Why?" Philip asked, equally blunt.

"Because he insulted me."

"You have insulted *me*," the deacon retorted. "They have lousy food, and I have told you many times, it must improve. The food they are eating is no good." The little money Philip was making from teaching, he was spending to buy supplemental food for the students.

"I am the abbot."

"And I am the dean of students," Philip shot back. "If you insist on this course of action, I will be leaving the school. I came here because I love the students and teaching our literature. But if I leave, I will tell the whole country of Lebanon what kind of life is being lived here."

"But he insulted me in front of the students," the abbot repeated.

"I will gather all of the students, and this young man will come and ask for your forgiveness in front of everyone and kiss your hand. And this will be done at once," Philip promised with a snap of his fingers.

The boy apologized, the food improved, and the problem was solved.

THE WILL TO WIN

"I loved being back at Balamand because I could do what I knew would work in reaching these students," Philip reminisces. "I coached the volleyball team, and I instilled in them the will to win. I told them, 'Men, we cannot lose. We don't want to lose as future leaders of the Church, we do not want to lose at volleyball. We are winners."

Where did Philip Saliba get this unyielding

will to keep moving ahead—and to win? Where along the way was that instilled in him?

"It was from my frustration with the Church and with our country. I wanted to create strong relationships, to build bridges that would span the gap I saw between the bishops and their clergy. My will to succeed was prompted as well by the chaos in the various governments of the Middle East during my upbringing. Our people lived in confusion. The Church is a part of society, and if society is chaotic, the Church is also chaotic. I wanted to help solve those problems.

"I very often asked myself in those early years, *Why can't it be better?* Look, St. Paul said that with Christ's help there is nothing we cannot do. We in the Church can shape history. Thus, I am permeated with idealism. I cannot just stand by. For this reason I often clashed with the Patriarch and the bishops."

He paused momentarily.

"I remember in 1949 when I was in Damascus. I often thought about changing our mode of dress. I knew historically that many years ago, when the clergy dressed in the black robe called the jibbe, they did not dress differently from the people. Except in Church, and then they wore their vestments. But outside they dressed like everybody else. If you look at the early iconography of the Church, our great saints like Basil or Gregory are dressed like everybody else, except in the Church.

The men, for example, had beards—secular or saint.

"But today, the Orthodox not only wear these black robes on the street, but now we've got the stovepipe hat. I hate it! I have no use for it. It is a symbol of tyranny, and we got it from the Turks!

"So I wrote an article on clergy dress and immediately caused a storm of protest. Bishops even wired the Patriarch. But that pressure didn't stop me then, and it won't stop me now. The fact is, these are false images. We can change the street dress of Orthodox clergy without changing the ethos of Orthodox Christianity."

As his year of residence at Balamand was winding down, the secretary of a consortium of English schools visited Lebanon and Philip had occasion to speak with him. He invited Philip to spend a year at one of the schools he represented and promised him a follow-up letter.

Philip was encouraged. He had always liked the Anglo-Saxon style of education. Impressed with Anglican priests and missionaries he met, he found them down to earth, friendly, genuine. They motivated him to study English history for himself, to read up on England's struggle for democracy.

Finally, the letter of formal invitation arrived. He could begin his work at Kelham College in Nottinghamshire, a poor village, still emerging from the ravages of World War II. The school would give him a scholarship for room, board, and tuition. But no money was available for travel.

When Philip received the letter he went directly to the Patriarch.

"I told you, I don't want you to do this," Alexander told him. "But if you must, do it on your own. I cannot give you money for the travel."

Then he paused and looked at his dejected deacon. "Just give me your best," Alexander said with a smile. "You may go."

Philip kissed his hand and thanked him. He left Damascus at once to visit his father and mother for a few days in Abou Mizan. Then he was off to England.

KELHAM

Kelham Theological School was a shock. To start with, the weather was horrible. It was typically the greyness and dampness of northern England. And this for a young man who, for the first time, leaves the glorious Mediterranean climate of Lebanon to move to a place where the sun doesn't shine! Every night Philip dreamed of sunlight. But every morning brought only the thick fog outside trying to get inside.

And it was cold. There was no central heat. Students brought coal into their rooms and struggled to keep their stoves lit. With coal heat, the walls were a dingy tannish-brown. Students did their own cooking, their own cleaning.

As at Balamand, the discipline at Kelham was very rigid. Students rose at five every morning, and a cold shower was the rule of the house. Philip went to see the dean. "In addition to this horrible weather, you want us to take a cold shower here in England? Can you exempt me, please?"

And he said, "No, no, this is the rule of the house."

Kelham was a Church of England college. The routine was to come for prayers seven times a day. Philip, like most of the other students, grew dissatisfied. "Many times I don't want to pray at all," he told his roommate. "I am sick of this. We can't just push a button and pray." At Kelham, they were trying to imitate monastic life, a very rigid rule of prayer.

On the plus side, Philip loved his study of English. Because of that, he made a conscious and specific decision to like the place. He used his free time for reading. In one class, he volunteered to translate some English prose into Arabic to become more at home with his work.

At both Christmas and Easter, the students had a month off from school. Philip received an invitation to spend his vacations with an English family. He was impressed with the way the English people lived and the good care they gave to their homes, their yards, and their gardens. Flowers surrounded every house, and green trees, tall and majestic, dominated the village neighborhoods and the countryside.

He also admired the patience of the English people. "If I get lost in the subway or the tube and

ask someone to help me, a stranger will stand there
as long as I need him to explain the directions to
me," he told his English host.

UNIVERSITY OF LONDON

After a year at Kelham, Philip said good-bye
to his instructors, his English family, and his fellow
students. He journeyed south to enroll at the University of London for the study of eighteenth- and
nineteenth-century English literature. Again, the
contrast to what he was used to at home was dramatic. But he did go from the cold rooms and cold
showers at Kelham to the very beautiful and cos-
mopolitan city of London. The university was a
personal challenge because he was intent upon
studying the literature he loved.

Whereas at Kelham Philip had been on
scholarship, in London he had to work. Though
he had partial aid, he signed on at a local restaurant as a waiter. And, while he liked his routine, he
had trouble making ends meet. So he turned to
simple pleasures. "I remember walking at night in
the London mist, often 'til three o'clock in the
morning, thinking and musing. I used to love to
stay up late and walk alone through those damp
and empty streets."

His year in London became a year of deep
personal crisis. As college students always have and
probably always will, Philip began to wrestle seriously with questions of his existence: *Who am I?*

Where am I going? Am I doing the right thing? But even more personal, exacting questions were running through Philip's mind: "Am I going to fulfill my commitment to the Church?" he would ask himself. "Here I am a deacon; I know what the Church is like on the inside. Can I work within this system? Can I be true to myself and produce what the bishops think I should?" Then he asked the ultimate question: "Will I survive spiritually? How will I survive?"

These were his "Church questions." But he had "world questions" too. Arab nationalism was back. The suffering of the people in his homeland was devastating to them, both during and after the war. Lebanon had been colonized for more than four hundred years under the Turks. When the Syrians and the Lebanese came to America in the nineteenth century they were even *called* Turks. After the collapse of the Ottoman Empire at the end of the First World War, instead of independence for Lebanon, Syria, and Palestine, France and Great Britain conspired to divide these countries. So Lebanon and Syria became French colonies; Palestine cast its lot with England and became a British colony.

In 1947, the United Nations partitioned Palestine, cordoning off the Jews from the Arabs. In 1948, the first Arab-Israeli war broke out and as a result 1.5 million Palestinians became dispossessed. Countless poverty-stricken Palestinian refugees were forced to leave their homes. They became displaced, exiled, barefooted, hungry, dirty. How could it be that a people who had lived in their own land for centuries—millennia—were suddenly gone? Before Abraham went to Palestine, they were there. They were the Philistines of the Old Testament, the indigenous people of the land. But now, suddenly, there was no country for them, no land. Deeply affected by the plight of his people, so many of them fellow Christians, Philip pondered and rethought the all-encompassing question of social justice.

"Wait a moment," Philip reasoned to himself. "Through a move toward nationalism, perhaps there could come social justice! All these Arab countries share the same culture. Why should they be divided? If you come to Syria, you arrive at the border, and there is a soldier standing guard. Who is he to say this border between Lebanon and Syria is impassable? Some kind of confederation might bring these countries together. The wealth of this land could be redistributed. Justly."

Then, another thought. "Where is the Church in all of this? Maybe we cannot deliver." In the idealism of his youth, Philip was becoming a nationalist.

But the basic questions still were not answered: *Who am I? Where did I come from? Where am I going?*

"In London I used to see question marks stretched all the way from Gloucester to the palace, from Trafalgar Square to the Tower Bridge. After a time, I started questioning nationalism too—and, the Church. Marxism, socialism, nationalism— what was the workable answer to the human condition, to life itself, to my dilemma?"

His thought patterns took a crosscurrent shift to *so what!* "So what if we buy into nationalism? So what if our people in these countries break out into unity and prosperity? Would we really solve our fundamental problems? Many countries of the world are unified and very wealthy, yet the people are still unhappy. What is their solution? They cry out over other problems: greed, inner rage, alienation. Even quiet desperation." Philip knew that nationalism could not speak to the ultimate condition of the human race.

"In my poverty, in my struggle with myself, I used to spend hours and hours in my room just thinking, meditating, and praying. I kept asking God to show me the way because I knew I was frustrated.

TURNING POINT

"I thank God that somehow He took me by the hand and led me to the right path. Through an impetus I cannot pinpoint, I became very much convinced that the only answer to one's problems is Jesus Christ. I remembered Jesus' words: 'I am the way, the truth, and the life.' And 'I am the Alpha and Omega, the beginning and the end.'"

Alone in London, away from Abou Mizan,

from Balamand, from Damascus, Philip could not leave off being Abdallah, the servant of God. "I made a firm resolution that the Church is my life and my future and that Jesus Christ is my Lord," he said years later. "I knew if I couldn't survive the pressures where I had been, maybe there was some place else on this earth where I could.

"Finally—it was like a light shining in all that darkness—I simply became convinced, very, very deeply convinced, that our personal struggles are never effectively addressed by the philosophies of men. Only in the Church can we find the justice, the equality, for which we yearn. But it has to be the Church as Christ wants it to be, not as we often practice. Institutionalism, pomposity, the aloofness of our leadership—that's not it!

"So I told myself I must do everything I can to stay in this Church, to serve the Lord, to work from within. Maybe we can change; somehow we must rediscover the real gospel, real apostleship, true patristic Christianity, and return to our birth at Pentecost. To help the Church be the Church as Jesus Christ wants it to be, without the man-made barriers, that became my dream."

And so Philip came to resolution, answers, peace in his renewed commitment to Christ.

A WORD TO THE WISE

But what about today, when college students come to him with similar frustrations? As they go through their own periods of doubt, or even rebellion, does that upset Philip the hierarch?

"As a matter of fact, I identify with them still. When people go through doubt and restlessness, I understand because I went through the same experience. These things do not worry me. What does worry me is indifference. There is nothing worse. As long as people are sincerely questioning, I don't mind at all if they come to me asking about the existence of God, about ritual, about the Church or our music. You don't like this? Fine. Let's talk about it."

He moved ahead in time. Shortly after he became bishop and moved to New York, a group of young people came to see him: "Your Eminence, we don't understand all these rituals that we have in Church. What's with all the symbolism?"

"Well, we don't have symbolism for symbolism's sake," he told them. "Every symbol in the Church points to a reality. I'll give you an example. The cross is a symbol. But the cross is the symbol of reality.

"Let me simplify things for you. Think of Christianity this way. Imagine a man, the Son of God, Jesus Christ, stretched out on a cross which extends from one end of the earth to the other. He embraces all of us. He loves you and He loves me enough to die to forgive our sins and give us new life."

They said, "Yes. We can imagine that."

"This is Christianity. This is the Church. And if you want to understand the symbolism that

we have in the Church, you have to become involved with Christ, the Lord of life and Head of the
Church. The cross helps us see that. The cross and
all the symbols that we have, all the services, point
to the reality of Jesus Christ."

Philip's dark night of the soul became his
deliverance, his renewed salvation, his willing surrender. Out of it, he came to love Christ more. And
he gained a new resolve to assume the role of
prophet for other strugglers like himself.

He is angered by evil, but compassionate
toward the world.

"We live in a most difficult time. When I was
growing up, we spent evenings at home with our
parents. We *talked* to each other. Today you visit
someone who has little children, and you rarely see
the children. They come home from school, and
they are lucky if mother is there to cook dinner.
After they do their homework, if they do their
homework, they are glued to the TV. They don't
talk with each other, and they don't talk with their
parents.

"Add to that the demonic influence in our
music, the movies, the raw pornography that dom-
inates our bookstores at the mall or the airport,
and you get a handle on why there is promiscuity in
our society.

"I enjoy television, but we were fortunate
to grow up without television and radio. We spent
our evenings as a family—talking, singing, sharing
whatever we had together."

The Church, he believes, must do everything possible to give young men and women priority—to show them love, to show them kindness and patience, to answer their deepest questions.

"Our most effective priests live and move with the young adults. They take them swimming, bowling, out on hayrides. They are able to converse with them, everything from questions about sex and marriage to the existence of God."

In Los Angeles not long ago, Philip held a fireside chat with a group of Orthodox college students. One of the girls asked him, "When you go to college, if you date a guy and you don't go to bed with him, he won't keep dating you. What should we do?"

"Dare to be different!" Philip exhorted her. "There is nothing wrong with being set apart from the girl next door. The girl next door is wrong. You are not a disposable item. A guy takes you to bed tonight, and tomorrow night it's somebody else, and the next night somebody else. You became a sex object, a commodity. Is that the kind of life you want to lead? Stick to your Christian values and you will never be sorry."

BACK TO BEIRUT

At the end of 1954 Philip Saliba returned to Beirut for a short time. Early the next year in Damascus he met the late Archbishop Samuel David of Toledo, Ohio, who would shortly invite him to

America. Philip and another close friend, Deacon Emile Hanna, served with Samuel David as he was visiting the patriarchate at the Cathedral of the Dormition in Damascus.

But for Philip there was still a conflict between the present and the future. Should he remain in Damascus, seek more education, prepare for something more?

After the liturgy that morning, Archbishop Samuel David asked Philip a pointed question: "Would you like to go with me to America?"

Philip thought for a moment. "On one condition," he answered. "Will you let me finish my theological education?"

CHAPTER

4

A Tale of Four Cities

By faith he sojourned in the
land of promise as in a
foreign country.

Hebrews 11:9

Throughout the twentieth century, Arab mothers developed a sense of anguish over their children's leaving home and coming to America. Their feelings were more than just intuitive; they were based on established fact.

If a son or a daughter were to sail off from Beirut for Athens or Paris to study, there were tears but no trauma. For the student would return one day to family and homeland. But not so with a journey to America. When a grown child embarked on that journey west, most often the voyage was for life.

When Deacon Philip left for London in 1953, his good-byes were never without hope of return. Late in 1955 the situation was markedly different. This time the destination was Boston, Massachusetts. Saleema knew this move might well be permanent. After all, her sister had left for America many years before and had not come back.

Philip, though, did not intend to depart for

good. When he left Shreen (the neighboring town
where the Saliba family had moved) on that cold
December day to study at Holy Cross in Boston, he
viewed the trip as nothing more than a year or two
of study abroad. In her heart, Saleema knew differently. And she was afraid. She had a strong, overwhelming sense that once her son left for America,
he would not come back to live in Lebanon again.

Elias held open the heavy black trunk lid of
the taxi cab while Philip loaded the last of his luggage. Tears flowed down Saleema's cheeks, and her
sobs were audible. Philip walked over and embraced her, holding her tight.

"Good-bye, Mother," he stammered, feeling
tears of his own well up in his eyes. He put to his
lips a handful of her soft black hair, which the
passing years had already generously graced with
gray. How he loved this woman who had given him
life nearly a generation before. "I will write," he
promised.

He held her out to arm's length before him
and managed a smile. "I love you, Mother," he
said. He turned, walked to the car, opened the pas-
senger door, and got in, pulling the door shut behind him.

The driver started the engine and had barely
begun to move forward, when Saleema grabbed
onto the car on Philip's side by the open window. "I
want to see you again," she cried out in anguish.
She looked directly into his eyes and ran alongside,

keeping pace with the moving car. "I want to see you again."

Then she released her hold, standing alone beside the road in the chilled morning air, weeping bitterly. "I want to see you again," Philip heard her cry out yet again as they drove away. It was a moment he would never forget.

BOSTON

Philip traveled to America with his close friend, Emile Hanna, who would one day be his fellow priest and serve the Antiochian archdiocese at St. Elijah Church in Ottawa, Ontario, Canada. Antoun Khouri met them in Beirut to say good-bye. Philip and Emile flew together to Athens, Greece, and spent New Year's Eve with friends who were in school there. On January 4, 1956, they landed in New York, and were driven on to Boston.

Since the 1930s Orthodox Christians in America under the Patriarch of Antioch had been split into two distinct factions. They lived in alienation from each other due to a hierarchical division. At Holy Cross, Philip and Emile Hanna were students under the sponsorship of Archbishop Samuel David of Toledo. Yet they were pleased to meet other students of Syrian or Lebanese descent under the archdiocese of New York led by Metropolitan Antony Bashir—men like Michael Azkoul,

George S. Corey, Louis Mahshie, Gregory Ofiesh, George Rados, Thomas Ruffin, and George Shaheen.

Holy Cross School of Theology, the Greek Orthodox seminary in America, occupies the acreage of a former private estate on a beautiful hilltop overlooking downtown Boston. It is situated in the upscale suburb of Brookline, just west of the city.

Most of the other students, of course, were from Greek family backgrounds and Greek Orthodox parishes. Many of the customs on campus were Greek as was most of the language spoken there. A few students from the Albanian Orthodox Church attended the school, plus an American convert or two. The struggle at Holy Cross was one of priorities: first to be Orthodox Christian and second to maintain Greek ethnic identity. Philip was deeply in love with the study of theology, and he was impressed with the academic resources at Holy Cross. But he and his friends were "the Syrians." Through both language and custom, the pressure was on to be Greek.

Father Georges Florovsky, a Russian Orthodox theologian of international reputation, was in residence at Harvard during those years, and he also taught at Holy Cross. For most of his years as a priest, he had been frustrated with the ethnic Orthodox situation in the New World. These feelings surfaced once again for him amidst reports that the seminary used the Greek language in some classes and chapel. "Boys," he announced one morning as he walked into class, "I think God gave the right faith to the wrong people!" The place dissolved in laughter.

Toward the end of the school year, a decision was made. Beginning with fall term, all classes would be taught in Greek. The second- and third-generation Greek Orthodox students faced the same problem as the non-Greek students: they knew only English.

"If I wanted to study Orthodox theology in Greek, I could have enrolled at the University of Thessalonica or at Athens," Philip complained to Emile Hanna. "But if the future of the Church is here in America, we need to learn to spread God's Word in English."

Faced with the impossibility of the situation, Metropolitan Antony Bashir of New York decided to take the students he oversaw out of classes at Holy Cross and transfer them to St. Vladimir's Seminary, the Russian Orthodox school, then located five blocks from Columbia University in New York City. There, English was used almost exclusively.

Archbishop Samuel David, on the other hand, was hesitant to make such a move. The resources in his archdiocese were severely limited, and one of his major benefactors was an elderly woman who also donated heavily to Holy Cross. Philip, along with Emile Hanna, requested a transfer with the others to St. Vladimir's.

"You have three choices," Archbishop Samuel David told his two young theologians. "You may stay at Holy Cross and study Christianity in the Greek language. Or, second, if you so choose, I will ordain you to the priesthood now and assign you to a parish out in the archdiocese. Third, you may return home."

Philip and Emile asked for a few moments to confer, to decide what to do. They liked none of the three choices.

"We are not going to stay at Holy Cross and be Grecophiles, we are not ready to be ordained, and we are certainly not going back to Lebanon," Philip told the archbishop.

"All right then," he said, "you are on your own."

Emile had relatives in Charleston, West Virginia, and he decided to stay for a while with them. Philip's aunt lived in faraway New Orleans, but with no reason to go there, he finished out the school year at Holy Cross and then asked a well-connected friend in Boston to help him find a job.

"How would you like to wait tables in a restaurant?" the friend asked.

"I wouldn't mind that," Philip responded. "I have done it before." A few nights later, he put on a clean white shirt and a starched white apron and began working as a waiter in a French restaurant.

The owner of the place was a merciless old French woman who took pleasure in browbeating her hired help. A waitress there had warned Philip of her heavy-handedness, so he made every effort to work fast and hard.

"I was very tolerant of the woman, heartless though she was, and I tried my best," he recalls. "My third night on the job, I was rushing around the dining area looking after my tables when she called me over."

"Monsieur Saliba, you are working very slow," she grumbled with her all-knowing air and one eyebrow lifted on high. The unmistakable look of forced termination was on her face.

Philip put the dishes down—on the floor! On his way out the door, he told the woman to keep his three days' pay for herself. "I don't want the money," he informed her.

He returned to his room, a hole in the wall in an old Boston tenement. Discouraged, suffocating in the heat of the humid summer night, and now unemployed, Philip took a pencil and a notepad, flung himself across his sagging bed, and composed a poem in Arabic—a satire of his working life in America entitled "Sweat." In eloquent verse it spoke emotionally of the inhumanity of man to man, especially the cruel way some employers treat their employees.

Emile Hanna loved the poem. He encouraged Philip to submit it to a newspaper. A short time later "Sweat" was published in the Arab-American paper, *Al-Samir*. Still burning with white-hot anger over the Syrian boys' departure from the seminary, the benefactress of Holy Cross spotted the poem. She notified the FBI! "This Saliba boy may be a Communist," she warned.

A few days later while Philip was in his rented cubicle poring over the want ads, looking for a job, there was a knock on the door. A tall man with a grim face and rimless eyeglasses told the bewildered young Lebanese student, "I'm from the FBI."

Philip gulped. "What do you want?"

"I want you to come with me to the office downtown," the man said mechanically. "We want to ask you some questions."

Grabbing his keys off the dresser, Philip followed the man down the long flight of stairs, through the front door, and out onto the street. He was shown to the back seat of a gray Chevrolet waiting curbside by the front door. Riding down the quiet tree-lined street, Philip muttered silently, "What else is going to happen to me here in the land of the free and home of the brave?"

"Have you ever been or are you now a member of the Communist Party?" asked the man behind the desk at the FBI central office.

"Me?" Philip answered nervously. "Never."

For a person from an Arabic country, nationalism and communism absolutely clash. You cannot affirm one, and at the same time affirm the other. The interrogation continued.

"Look," Philip said, now more firmly. "For a time, I was a nationalistic sympathizer. But I had no use for communism at all. I never have had. It is against everything I believe in. Check my records. I have nothing to do with communism."

After three solid hours of questioning, Philip was told he was free to leave. Left on the street to take a series of long bus rides home, Philip was never to be contacted by the FBI again.

Next morning, Philip called the friend who had gotten him in as a waiter. "I lost my job the other day, and I need another one," he said. "I'd like something better."

"There's this job at a factory . . . . A Syrian man owns it."

"I wouldn't mind that," Philip said.

The job paid fifty dollars a week, a decent wage in Boston in 1956.

In the meantime, Philip began thinking ahead about continuing his education. Wayne State University in Detroit came to mind. A number of friends back in Lebanon had gone there. He applied for and received a scholarship.

DETROIT

At the end of the summer Philip moved to Michigan, checked the phone book, and visited the Antiochian Orthodox parish, St. George's. The priest, Father Anthony Wolf, welcomed the young, available, energetic deacon. The parish board, at its regular meeting, invited him to serve on a regular basis.

Whereas Philip was in America under Archbishop Samuel David of Toledo, St. George was a part of the archdiocese of New York. Appropriate phone calls were made to arrange for a transfer. "By all means, take Philip under your jurisdiction," Archbishop Samuel David told Metropolitan Antony Bashir.

It was a bright day for Philip. Here he was, enrolled on scholarship at Wayne State University, a deacon at St. George's, and now part of the archdiocese of New York. Virtually all his credits from his past education were accepted, and he enrolled as a junior at Wayne State in the fall of 1956.

On campus, there was an active chapter of the Orthodox Christian Fellowship, OCF. Philip became a regular, and, before the fall term was out, he was elected president. Students from Greek, Russian, Serbian, and Antiochian backgrounds were part of OCF. By winter, over two hundred Orthodox students were meeting each week.

"One day as I was riding the bus from campus back to the church," Philip recalls, "I saw this billboard advertising a new motion picture, *And God Created Woman,* starring an actress I had never heard of before, Brigitte Bardot. Only in America, I reasoned, would you have a movie with a biblical theme playing in a theater. I couldn't imagine a religious film being advertised on a billboard."

The OCF group was meeting that night on

Above: Metropolitan Philip's home parish, St. George, in Abou Mizan, Lebanon.

Below: Student days at Balamand. Philip is at right, Antoun Khouri, left, Bishop Sergios, lower center. The late Father Michael Howard is next to Philip.

*Philip Saliba at 14 in 1945,
Balamand Seminary.*

*George Shaheen, Philip, George
Rados, Emile Hanna at Holy Cross
Seminary in January, 1956.*

*College senior, 1958,
Wayne State University.*

*Father Philip, pastor, 1962,
St. George Church, Cleveland.*

Archbishop Philip Saliba, chanting the Gospel at the service of his consecration, August 14, 1966, St. Elias Monastery, near Dhour Cheweir, Lebanon.

The presentation of the bishop's crown to Philip at his consecration by Patriarch Theodosius VI. In the center is Bishop Ignatius, dean of Balamand, the present Patriarch of Antioch.

The newly consecrated Philip holds the Cross for veneration by the faithful at the close of the Divine Liturgy.

*Above: reception with Patriarch
Theodosius VI after the consecration
of Metropolitan Philip. Metropolitan
Ilyas Kurban is behind Philip.*

*Right: the hands of Metropolitan Philip at
the breaking of the Eucharistic bread.*

The Enthronement of Metropolitan Philip, October 13, 1966, at St. Nicholas Cathedral, Brooklyn, New York. On the left is Archbishop Iakovos, primate of the Greek Orthodox Church in North and South America. At far right is Father Theodosius Lazar, now Metropolitan Theodosius of the Orthodox Church in America.

Upper left: with Lyndon Johnson, 1968.

Above: with Dwight Eisenhower during his retirement, 1968.

Center left: with Jimmy Carter and Patriarch Elias, 1977.

Lower left: with Ronald Reagan, 1982.

Father Alexander Schmemann, Father Ellis Khouri, Bishop Elia Saliba with the Metropolitan in 1974.

A 1977 meeting of the Standing Conference of Orthodox Bishops in America (SCOBA) included, left to right, Metropolitan Philip, Archbishop Iakovos and Metropolitan Theodosius.

the Wayne State campus. Philip decided to take them all to the movie, making the outing a group project. The students arrived on time, paid at the door, and were in their seats for the opening curtain.

"Before any time at all had elapsed, here was Bardot baring almost all—just what a group of single young men need, right?" Philip recalls with embarrassment.

"Hey, what is this movie, Philip?" some of the sophomore men snickered. "You said this was a movie about Genesis?"

They laughed him to scorn, and he laughed with them. He had fallen for what even the secular reviewers had dubbed as a "continental peep show." It was time to concentrate on the study of English idioms and their alternate meanings in Hollywood.

Wayne State was a crossroads for Philip Saliba. Particularly impressed with American history, he was taken with the American Revolution. And learning of Thomas Jefferson's concept that democracy is not just for the people in America, but for the people of the whole world, Philip came to believe that under democratic rule people in the Middle East could break the chains that enslaved them. Youthful idealism began to well up in him again.

"I had a marvelous time at Wayne State. Besides my scholarship, I was paid seventy-five dollars a month by the church for helping the priest do the liturgical services. I kept the books there, too, and typed the bulletin. Thank God for that seventy-five dollars a month."

St. George's, Detroit, an ethnic congregation of self-starting immigrant people, is typical of the Arabic Orthodox Church in America. The people extended constant hospitality to the new deacon; he was besieged by nice elderly mothers with offers of home-cooked meals and plenty of old-country warmth. An international student in the New World couldn't ask for more.

While Philip was in school in Detroit in 1958, a cable arrived from Damascus. Patriarch Alexander III, the man who had formed him in the diaconate, had passed away. Patriarch Theodosius VI was chosen to succeed him as the new head of the Antiochian See.

Philip graduated with a B.A. in history early in 1959. Soon, Metropolitan Antony was on the phone, long distance from New York. "Now that you have graduated from the university, I need your help as a priest at St. George Church in Cleveland."

"Detroit already asked me to be a priest, Your Eminence," Philip said, "and I refused. The reason is, I am not ready yet."

"You are not ready? When are you going to be ready?" the metropolitan countered.

"I don't know. I am still young."

Antony was very insistent. "You are a deacon now, and you are not going to get married, isn't that correct?"

"Yes, Your Eminence," Philip answered.

"This archdiocese needs you," Antony repeated.

The metropolitan knew of Philip's background, that he had served well at Balamand, that he had been secretary to the Patriarch. "You have a tremendous future," Antony told him.

Philip knew the priesthood would be a momentous step for him. Earlier in life he had made up his mind that he wanted to serve the Church, and now the archbishop was pressing him into action. This would be his personal dying with Christ.

Before he decided on Cleveland, a delegation from St. George drove up to visit him. "How much money do you want?" they asked.

"I don't care," Philip answered. "Whatever you give me is fine. You are good people, and I want to serve you. I will be your father, and you will certainly not starve me to death."

The idea of a priest bartering for a paycheck was foreign to this immigrant. And it was foreign to traditional Orthodox Christianity. "I wish I could impress this on our people," Philip says. "The first question is never how much the priest wants to be paid. Besides, the more he asks for, the less he receives!"

On March 1, 1959, Metropolitan Antony ordained Philip Saliba to the holy priesthood to serve in Cleveland. At his ordination, the new priest was honest with his listeners:

In 1948, I left the Balamand Seminary and its quiet life and returned to society and its problems. Thus, an era of doubt, anxiety, and rebelliousness began in my life.

During this period, I lost some of my faith in the Church because I could not differentiate between the Church as a human institution subject to sins and tribulations, and the Church as a divine institution for which Christ died and was resurrected.

Tormented by doubt, despair and confusion, I found refuge in some secular religions. But it was not long before God visited me and said, "Rise and stand on your feet; for I have appeared to you for this purpose, to make you a minister and a witness both of the things which you have seen and of the things which I will yet reveal to you" (Acts 26:16).

Thus, I returned to Christ to find in Him the right answer—not only to my personal problems, but also to the problems of humankind and history.

CLEVELAND

The people at St. George were delighted to have Philip in Cleveland. But shortly after his arrival, the new priest faced a problem no pastor ever expects or believes will happen. For reasons unknown to anyone, an elderly man in the congregation publicly demanded his dismissal.

"What is your problem?" Philip asked. There was no reply.

"He has no use for me at all," Philip explained at his first meeting with the parish council. "He doesn't even know me."

A few days later someone called, reporting that the critic had just been admitted to the hospital. Immediately, Philip left his office, taking another member of the parish with him. Enroute to the medical center, Philip, knowing the man was sick and weak, determined to be compassionate. As he stepped inside the doorway of the hospital room, Philip noted on the man's face a softness he had not seen a few days earlier.

"I have come to pray for you," Philip said.

"Okay," the man whispered.

"I prayed for him from the depth of my heart," Philip said years later. "Sometimes you feel that the Holy Spirit is moving through you in an unusual way. I knew God would do something merciful for us." Healed of his sickness, the man went on to become a loyal stalwart in the Church.

Philip learned early to spend himself as a minister to the sick, to be there for the grieving, to share in people's joys and sorrows. Enjoying every moment of his work, he kept his house open day and night to the teenagers, the choir, the parish council, and the ladies' society.

"I had one lady who loved to talk with me. I soon discovered that if there was some good news I wanted spread through the parish I could call her

and say, 'I have something confidential to tell you.'
Five minutes later I would try her phone and it
would be busy. And it would stay busy all day
long."

Shortly after Philip moved to Cleveland, An-
toun Khouri, now Deacon Antoun, came to New
York to attend seminary at St. Vladimir's. One day,
Philip called his close friend. "I miss seeing you,"
Philip told Antoun. "Come visit me in Cleveland."

"How do I get there?" Antoun asked, not yet
knowing his way around the United States. It was
reminiscent of their first encounter at Balamand.

"It's easy," Philip assured him. "Just go to
downtown Manhattan to the Greyhound Bus de-
pot, buy a ticket to Cleveland, and you're set."

"How long a trip is it?" Antoun asked.

"You'll be here in a few short hours," Philip
told him. Antoun assumed that meant two hours,
three at the most. He boarded the bus at eight the
next evening and expected to arrive at eleven, and
be in bed by midnight.

An hour passed, then two. He had already
gone up front twice to ask the distance to Cleveland. It was pitch black outside as the bus rolled on
through the eastern Pennsylvania hills. Midnight
came and went. "What is going on here?" Antoun
asked himself.

"Wilkes-Barre," the driver called out at one-
thirty in the morning. "We'll take a twenty-minute
break."

"Is this near Cleveland?" Antoun asked him.

"Look, Mister, it's a long way to Cleveland," he snapped.

At four-thirty, Antoun walked again to the front of the coach. "Where are we?"

"Lock Haven," grumbled the driver. "You sit down and get some sleep. We'll be there sooner if you quit talking to me."

"I've never heard of Lick Haven," Antoun complained as he stumbled back to his seat.

"Du Bois," the driver yelled out at 5:50 A.M. Only the sleepless, antagonized Antoun was awake to hear him. Daylight broke to reveal a scene of cattle and countryside.

By seven o'clock a large city was in the distance. Antoun grabbed his bag, stepped up to the first seat, but said nothing. He looked at the driver expectantly. "Relax," said the driver. "It's Youngstown."

It was after eight when they finally pulled into downtown Cleveland. Barely awake, frustrated, and nearly incoherent, Antoun was first out the door, almost losing his footing on a grease spot on the garage floor. Inside the terminal there was no Philip.

Antoun dialed his number. "Where are you?" he moaned to Philip. "Why aren't you here to pick me up?"

"Be patient!" Philip said in Arabic, as he smiled over his morning coffee. "There's a taxi outside. Have him bring you to the church on West 14th Street."

Antoun hit the roof. But what could he do? He hung up the phone and hailed a cab.

The moment he saw Philip, they embraced, and Antoun forgot all about the harrowing bus ride. "If I'd told you the distance from New York to Cleveland, you'd never have come," Philip grinned as they walked into the church. At the end of their ten-day visit, Philip bought him a plane ticket back to New York.

In Cleveland, Philip's most ambitious task was the building of a new educational center, the largest in the archdiocese. He first approached the priests of the other Orthodox parishes in town about making it a pan-Orthodox effort, available to all.

"If we develop a parochial school, will you send your children to it?" Father Philip had asked the other priests.

"Yes, of course," they encouraged him.

The building was designed with seventeen classrooms, a gym including lockers and showers for boys and girls, plus a large meeting room. Money for the center, a $300-thousand project built during 1961 and 1962, was donated by the people of St. George's. But when school was ready to begin in the fall, the other priests had changed their minds. "We're not ready to move ahead at this time," they said. The dream was tempered with reality.

"Then we'll rent it to the Cleveland schools," Philip decided. The board of education signed a lease for daytime use of the facility for $50 thousand a year. In the evenings, Father Philip conducted a series of lectures on Orthodox theology for Christian education workers in the city. Though the series was highly successful, the young priest's dream of launching a full-scale parochial school was never realized.

The early 1960s were the strong and fruitful years of Metropolitan Antony Bashir's leadership of the archdiocese. Tireless and visionary, he was a dynamic worker and communicator. He had built a number of new parishes across the country, inspired gifted young men to prepare for the priesthood, and even talked of beginning a seminary to serve the archdiocese. But his immediate need was for an auxiliary bishop to assist him with administrative matters. To Father Philip's surprise, the metropolitan approached him.

"Why talk with me about needing a bishop?" Philip asked.

"Well, in thinking about your work here in . . . ."

"Remember the constitution of the patriarchate, Your Eminence," Philip interrupted, "the section on educational requirements. I have no degree in Orthodox theology, only my undergraduate degree, and I cannot be consecrated."

Even with the year at Holy Cross and the theological courses he had taken both in Damascus and in England, he still lacked a year of work to complete a master's of divinity.

"We'll see about that," Metropolitan Antony said softly.

NEW YORK CITY

Fall 1964 began a year of sabbatical for Philip Saliba. Father George Simon, a retired priest living in Cleveland, was asked to serve in Philip's absence. Philip promised to go back during Christmas and Easter to conduct services.

After his years of hard work to get through undergraduate school and then serving the parishes in Detroit and Cleveland, a year at St. Vladimir's without the pressure of pay-as-you-go outside work was a welcomed break. Philip thrived on theology, Bible, liturgics, and Church history under such fine professors as Veselin Kesich, John Meyendorff, and Alexander Schmemann.

In February, a telegram arrived from Lebanon: "Your mother, Saleema, has fallen asleep in Christ." In Middle Eastern custom, the dead are buried almost immediately, and therefore loved ones abroad do not return home. Composing himself, Philip had an overriding desire to talk about her, to put his love for her into words. He telephoned Najib, now an undergraduate at Miami University in Ohio. The two brothers held a memorial to their mother over long distance, remembering their childhood with her and giving thanks to God for her example and her life.

Philip's years as a deacon and a parish priest

molded his approach to classroom theology. There appeared to him to be a gaping hole, an absence of application of his seminary courses to the needs of his people. His friendship with Father Alexander Schmemann was strong, and he went to see him.

"There is something lacking here," Philip began boldly. "Have you ever served a parish?"

"Personally, I have not," Father Alexander said. "All of us here go out and serve somewhere on Sunday, but just a few of the faculty have been full-time priests."

"We've got to bring the Orthodox Church from Byzantium to America," Philip argued. "Centuries ago, people discussed theology in the marketplace—the two natures in Christ, the heresy of Arius, the procession of the Holy Spirit from the Father."

"The golden age of Christendom," Father Schmemann added.

"I am learning our Orthodox heritage so well here at St. Vlad's," Philip said. "But those golden days are long past. In our time, people have different problems. A half-billion people go to bed hungry every night. Here in America we have problems of drugs—and what about these countless broken families?

"Or how do you deal with freedom?" Philip went on. "There was a time when people rebelled because of lack of freedom and lack of bread. But today—look at our campuses. People are rebelling because of too much freedom, too much bread."

Father Schmemann nodded yes.

"Father Alexander, we need pastoral theology here at seminary. We have to learn to apply the Bible to these needs, apply it to life. Man is more than a concept. He is flesh and blood. He has ideas and values, standards of good and evil. We must bring our Orthodox theology from its ivory tower and make it understandable to our people *today*."

Philip knew he was on a crusade. If Christian theologians and priests could not adequately present Jesus Christ to a teenager with a drug problem or to a mother trying to put together a broken home, who would do it? To this very day, in his efforts on behalf of American converts and seekers, he continues to press the same point he argued with Father Schmemann in 1964—to make Orthodox theology "people friendly" without watering it down.

From time to time Philip would break from his studies to eat lunch at Nathan's, a popular restaurant near the seminary. One noon, he met some new immigrants from Jordan who were working in the kitchen. Some were Orthodox Christians, and others called themselves Latins. Here, without planning it, he was handed an opportunity to bring Orthodox Christianity to some new people, a chance to practice what he preached. "Where do you go to church?" Philip asked.

"Once a year or so we go to St. Nicholas Cathedral in Brooklyn," they said.

"Don't you have an Orthodox Church here?" Father asked.

"No, we don't."

"Well, what would you think if we started a Church here?" Philip challenged.

"That's a marvelous idea," one man answered, "but we want everything in Arabic."

Philip said. "With forty families, we could have a Church. Let's do something about it."

The following Saturday morning, Philip drove across town to see Metropolitan Antony in Brooklyn.

"I found some Orthodox families in Yonkers," Philip began.

"Good work," the bishop replied.

"Let us build a Church for them."

"Don't bother," he said. "These people are not serious about the Church."

"Then, please, just give me permission to work with them."

"Fine," he said, "if you want to waste your time."

Philip was delighted with the opportunity. He got in touch with the people, and they agreed to get their friends together for a meeting. Each week they spent their evenings in various homes, with Philip leading the discussion.

Some of them wanted to hear Arabic poetry, so he was there to recite Arabic poetry. Others wanted to hear Arabic chanting; he chanted for them. Like Christ with the woman at the well, he started where they were. Slowly, he found himself establishing a firm and vital relationship with this community. A love affair between pastor and people was under way.

One spring evening in 1965 Philip had an announcement. "It is time to start a Church. And to start a Church, we are going to need money. So how do you want to go about it?"

"Why don't we start by making pledges?" someone suggested.

Within a few weeks the little group raised enough money to buy a vacant church. They moved at once into the facility and Father Philip and others he recruited to help from St. Vladimir's began leading services. Growing together as a community in Christ, they formed a lasting parish, celebrating their twenty-fifth year as St. Mary's Church, Yonkers, New York, in 1990, a parish of some 150 souls pastored full time by Father Michael Khoury.

Just before registration ended for the spring semester, Archbishop Antony sent a student he had met in a seminary in Brooklyn to enroll at St. Vladimir's. Philip agreed to take the new student under his wing, but he could not understand why the metropolitan had sent him there. For however loudly people spoke, the student could not hear them. He had attended seminary classes for nearly a month before his severe hearing impairment was discovered. A frustrated Father Schmemann finally put in a call to the archbishop.

"Your Eminence," Father Schmemann said, "this new student of yours cannot follow the lectures."

"What did you say?" Metropolitan Antony asked.

"He can't hear very well."

"Did you say he does not hear you well?" Antony teased, raising his voice.

Father Alexander had taken the bait. He was had, and he knew it. "That is what I said," Father Alexander muttered. "He does not hear what people say to him."

"Well, that's exactly the kind of priest I need," laughed Antony victoriously as he replaced the receiver on the hook.

With final exams and his master's thesis behind him, Philip received his master's of divinity degree at the June graduation ceremony in Crestwood and returned home to Cleveland a few days later to resume his ministry at St. George's.

CHAPTER

5

Changing of the Guard

For a bishop must be blameless, as a steward of God, not self-willed, not quick-tempered, not given to wine, not violent, not greedy for money, but hospitable, a lover of what is good, sober-minded, just, holy, self-controlled, holding fast the faithful word as he has been taught, that he may be able, by sound doctrine, both to exhort and convict those who contradict.

Titus 1:7–9

I t was a cold and blustery winter morning in early February 1966. Philip had just walked into his office at the church and set his briefcase on a chair when the phone rang.

"Good morning, St. George Church," he said as he answered. "This is Father Philip."

It was Metropolitan Antony phoning from a hospital room in Boston. "How do you feel?" the archbishop asked weakly.

"I am fine," Philip answered. "But what about you? How do you feel?"

For the first time in Philip's memory, the response of the archbishop was negative. "I don't feel well," he admitted. In a moment a man perceived to be immortal had put on mortality. "I don't feel well at all, and I might have to remain in the hospital."

It was the last time Philip was to hear his voice.

Metropolitan Antony Bashir lived fourteen days in the hospital and died on February 15, 1966, of cancer of the lymph glands. Ever the shepherd who served, who disdained having others wait on him, he had managed to keep his illness a secret.

His death brought shock waves throughout the archdiocese and the Orthodox world. So robust in his stature, in his magnetism and constant enthusiasm, this dedicated worker was expected by the people who knew and loved him to go on almost forever at the helm of the Church. Suddenly, he was gone.

"He was perhaps the most dynamic preacher of the gospel I ever heard in my entire life," Philip told a long-time friend at the funeral. "And what a tremendous sense of humor."

Coming from Lebanon at a time when the country was in severe economic straits, Archbishop Antony had learned to be tight with his money. Hesitant to hire secretarial help, he handled all his own office work, typed his own letters, and kept few records or files. To save archdiocesan funds, he often phoned people collect. When a priest heard a long distance operator say, "I have a collect call for you," the priest would join her for the rest of the sentence, "from a Metropolitan Antony in Brooklyn." His normal phone bill each month was $8.

"In order to conserve paper, he would turn the page over in the typewriter and type on the back," Philip recalled. "He never spent money on himself or even on his friends. He knew no personal luxury. He just saved everything."

His clergy loved him. The laity could never

praise him enough. Busy executives, laborers, homemakers, people with no room in their schedules for interruptions dropped everything they were doing and traveled to New York for his funeral.

Among the clergy, there was an unsettling sense of despair. "For a moment we all forgot the Church was not built on Antony—or Athanasius or Peter or Paul," Philip remembered. "We had to come back to the realization it was built upon Christ Himself."

The day before the funeral, the clergy met to make assignments for the service. The Right Reverend Ellis Khouri was dean of the clergy *(protosyngelos)* and was assumed to be the one to deliver the sermon at the service. But it was he who led a delegation of priests who came to Philip and said, "You speak."

"I will sing. I will chant the prayers," Philip said.

"No way," they insisted. "You speak."

Philip hesitated again.

"You must do it," they said.

On a wind-chilled February day, the beloved archshepherd Antony was committed to his eternal rest at Greenwood Cemetery, on a hill overlooking Brooklyn, the city of his labors for most of his adult years. A spirit of sadness enveloped the crowd as hundreds of men and women departed the graveside in bewilderment, uncertain of the future of an Orthodox archdiocese that had just begun to take root in the fertile American soil.

The mourning would go on for forty days.

THE NOMINATION: NEW YORK CITY

By early March it was time to think about Metropolitan Antony's successor. On March 16, 1966, some three hundred parish representatives from the archdiocese, both clergy and laity, gathered at the Sheraton Hotel in New York City. In the polity of the Antiochian Church, the tradition is for three men to be chosen by the people. Then, unless there is good reason not to do so, one of the three is elected bishop by the Patriarch and his Holy Synod.

Presiding over the nominations was Metropolitan Ilyas Kurban, the *locum tenens,* or temporary substitute, sent by the Patriarch of Antioch, Theodosius VI. His role was to act as primate until a new bishop was selected. Arriving from Damascus, he would stay on in North America until an orderly transition under the new metropolitan could be made. At the nomination, he was to call each session to order and run the meeting according to the traditions of the Church and the patriarchal and archdiocesan constitutions.

At the opening session, all who were eligible by reason of age, education, discipline of celibacy, and record of service would be asked to say something of an autobiographical nature to the assembly. One of the candidates had come to New York with a carefully prepared brochure including a picture of himself, his life story, and a listing of his various academic degrees. He campaigned aggressively in the hotel lobby, passing out his leaflet and working the crowd.

Philip made a conscious decision not to campaign, to remain inconspicuous. As he relaxed alone in his room on the day before those eligible were to speak, the phone on his bedside table rang. It was Father Paul Romley, dean of St. Nicholas Cathedral in Los Angeles, calling from the lobby.

"The delegation from Los Angeles would like to meet with you, Father. We want you to come down to the lobby." The group from L.A. was the largest single delegation to come to New York.

"What do you mean?" Philip replied.

"The West Coast people want to get to know you," Father Paul continued.

"Fine, they can come to my room. There is enough space here for some of them to sit, the rest to stand. But I'm not coming down to the lobby to campaign—for anything."

Up the stairs and elevators they all came, eager to meet and visit with a man they felt would be a leading candidate.

The following morning, one by one, the candidates stood to speak. It was a difficult assignment to come to the podium and objectively try to extol one's own virtues; rehearse personal accomplishments, goals, degrees, and diverse qualifications; and then sit back down. The candidates stepped forward to speak according to the alpha-

betical order of their last names. Saliba was the final name on the ledger.

When his turn to speak came, Philip began
by motioning to the other candidates and with a
chuckle urging his hearers to "vote for them because they are all highly qualified and I am the
chief among sinners."

Then he got more serious.

"It is not our degrees, really, that make us
qualified. A man can have all the right academic
credentials from the great centers of learning the
world over, but without the grace of God he'll never
be able to do the job. This is why in the service of
ordination we pray, 'O God, be favorably pleased
to grant to him the great grace of Your Holy Spirit,
and make him wholly Your servant, in all things
acceptable to You.'" He repeated again this prayer
from the service of ordination, this time in Arabic.

The crowd began to murmur, "He knows
Arabic well, and he can handle English too." Philip
finished his remarks and took his seat.

Metropolitan Kurban rose to oversee the
voting. Philip reasoned silently, "If this is the will of
God—and not what I want or don't want—if this is
a challenge He's putting before me, I'll not say no
to Him."

Here he was, at thirty-five, a recently ordained priest, barely old enough even to qualify, an
immigrant son of a Lebanese farmer, being considered for metropolitan of New York and all North
America. Inside, he trembled. But his life had al-

ready been one of dreaming unlikely dreams and
exercising bold courage. If he felt a certain path
was the will of God, he would give that challenge
everything he had.

The voting seemed to move very slowly:
counting, recounting; checking, rechecking. Finally, Metropolitan Kurban stood to speak. "There
are three nominees. Bishop Ignatius Hazim has
been nominated as has Father Gregory Aboud.
Father Philip Saliba from St. George, Cleveland, is
our third nominee with 260 votes."

Philip could not believe his ears. He remained in his chair dazed and in shock. He was not
sure he would even be nominated, much less receive such an overwhelming majority of votes. The
mandate was given, and the choice of the faithful
was clear.

The slate of candidates was ready to be submitted to the Holy Synod at the patriarchate of
Antioch.

THE SYNOD

It was a supremely difficult time in the history of the Church of Antioch. The Holy Synod
(about sixteen men in all) was hopelessly divided,
or at least nearly so. The same body that sent out
Paul and Barnabas as apostles nearly two thousand
years earlier, was today disunified in purpose and
split in ecclesiastical loyalties.

There were bishops under Antioch who

held a great allegiance to the Patriarch of Moscow and another group closely allied with the Greek Patriarch of Constantinople. The Church was divided as the world was divided. It was after all, 1966, the apex of the era of the cold war.

Philip was beholden to neither Moscow nor Constantinople. His commitment was to discern and do the will of God. Nonetheless, he found himself in the middle of a swirling controversy. The whispered charge against him was arresting for any immigrant: "He is an *American!*"

At the patriarchate in Damascus, what would they do? The choice was clearly not from among the three candidates from the new world. For many had predicted the synod would reject the whole nomination process and, with it, the entire slate. Political game playing appeared to be the order of the day.

Metropolitan Kurban, who had presided over the nomination process, was himself a part of the Holy Synod of Antioch and was known as a forthright and honorable man. When he returned to Damascus with the recommendation of the Orthodox faithful in America, he was very outspoken.

"Everything was done above board," he told his fellow synod members. "If you reject this slate and call for another nomination, you will get the same result in a second election. This is the will of the people, both the clergy and the laity. What will you do with this recommendation?"

The metropolitan took a firm stand to support the nominations in New York as did the future Patriarch of Antioch, Bishop Ignatius. Though Ignatius was not at that time on the synod, he was in a position of influence as dean of Balamand Seminary.

The opposition was not aimed specifically at Philip, but at the slate in general and the nomination process itself. For whoever would be chosen metropolitan would be added *de facto* to this synod, and the balance of power between the pro-Moscow and pro-Constantinople forces was precarious.

A priest whom Philip had helped to stay in America was now back in the Middle East, spreading malicious rumors through the synod about Philip's character and qualifications. Soon, letters began to circulate impugning the integrity of Philip and the other nominees. The disunity and disarray of the synod in Damascus was, like a disease, contagious. It spread to North America.

By early July 1966, after four months of deliberation, no decision had yet been reached in Damascus, no vote even attempted. Metropolitan Kurban, who had returned to the United States as *locum tenens,* stayed in communication with the Patriarch and members of the synod. There was no apparent movement in any direction.

The priests in America were becoming restless. A call came from Archimandrite Ellis Khouri from St. Nicholas Church in Grand Rapids, Michigan, to Father Philip at St. George, Cleveland. "A group of our clergy would like you to go with us to Damascus."

"Do you know what you're asking?" Philip replied.

"Metropolitan Kurban is going back to Damascus at the end of July because the synod is going to meet," Father Ellis continued. "Our clergy want to send a delegation to the meeting to impress upon the synod that what happened in the March nominations is the will of the people. They should not bother to reject our nominees and find some new ones because the result will be the same. We are going, and we want you with us."

"Please, Father," Philip reasoned, "this is the worst thing I could do. If I go, everyone will say I'm there to buy my way into office. God forbid!"

"But, Father. . . ."

"This would be absolutely the worst thing I could do," Philip repeated. "Whatever the Lord wills, may His will be done. If you want to go to represent the archdiocese, I cannot stop you. But for me to go with you—forgive me—I will not go."

"Look, Father Philip, you can't say no to a group of . . ."

"It is not wise for me to go," Philip said firmly.

". . . to a group of priests who are going at their own expense." Father Ellis finished his sentence anyway, though he and Philip both knew continued pleading would be to no avail.

Not many days later, the delegation of priests headed by Father Ellis Khouri and including Fathers George S. Corey, Antony Gabriel, George Ghannam, George Rados, Thomas Ruffin, Joseph Shaheen, and Theodore Ziton and a layman from Indianapolis, Michel Kafoure, boarded a plane in New York headed for London, then Beirut. They registered at the Bristol Hotel. From there they drove to St. Elias Monastery where the conclave would be held.

THE AUGUST STORM

Some of the bishops on the patriarchal synod had been heavily influenced by communism. In the zeal of this group to stand with the Patriarch of Moscow and the piety of the Russian Orthodox faithful, they had come to see communism as a legitimate governmental philosophy with which the Church could coexist. While it was difficult to determine how or why this kind of attachment to Marxism had developed, rumor was that these men had made a number of trips to Russia in the late '50s and early '60s, and that the Moscow patriarchate had been extremely kind to them.

Predictably, the American delegation immediately ran headlong into the Moscow bloc of influence on the synod in Damascus. Philip's history of outspoken criticism of Marxist doctrine and his related denunciation of those in the Russian Church who had been captivated or romanced by communism were taking an obvious toll on his chances for election. "He's too big over there," one of the opposition bishops complained. "He works for the Pentagon!"

"The presence of our American clergy delegation made a statement to Damascus: *We are interested in you*," said Father George Corey, looking back. "In all honesty, there was not good rapport between the patriarchate and the American Church in the middle third of this century. They felt we really did not care."

There was a firm wall of opposition, with vehemence, determined to turn back the nominees at all costs—and most especially, Philip Saliba. It was now the beginning of August, and a storm with the potential of shattering the Antiochian Church in America was brewing. The American priests took a day out to fly down to Jerusalem to pray at the Church of the Holy Sepulcher.

As the first days of August wore on, the delegation from America stepped up its efforts to phone or visit personally with each member of the synod. Most of the delegation favored Philip's election, but the impetus of their efforts was aimed at calling the synod to confront the nomination itself and choose a primate for North America. Their trips across town from the hotel to the monastery and to the homes and offices of the bishops on the synod who lived in various parts of Lebanon and Syria seemed too many to count. Short nights of sleep and long hot summer days were taking a toll on the American priests.

By August 5, with no apparent results from their visit, the American delegation departed for home, leaving from the Beirut airport. They were dejected. Believing they had done all they could, they felt that very little had been gained. Would a decision ever be forthcoming? And if so, what would it be? Only God knew.

But as the American priests were en route home, events suddenly turned. Their presence in Lebanon and Syria had not been in vain. After a lengthy deliberation the morning of August 5, the opposition to the American nominees became a minority within the synod. The opposing bishops withdrew from their efforts to turn the request of the North American Church away.

The stage was set for a vote. On the evening of August 5, on the eve of the Feast of the Transfiguration of the Son of God—the feast day on which Philip was made deacon—the blockade within the synod of Antioch dissolved, and the voting was under way.

The telephone rang at St. George Church, Cleveland. It was a person-to-person call from St. Elias Monastery to Father Philip Saliba. Patriarch Theodosius VI himself was on the line. "My son, Philip, you are to be the bishop to succeed Antony."

By the next morning, the parish phone would not stop ringing. Malveena "Beans"

Molnar, a selfless lady in the congregation, volunteered to handle the calls. She began the day by changing the greeting from the customary "Good morning, St. George Church," to "Hello, Bishop-elect's office."

Meantime, Father Ellis Khouri and the other priests in the American delegation stumbled off the plane at New York's Kennedy Airport mid-morning on August 6, after a grueling nine-hour flight from Heathrow. "Let me give Father Philip a call," he told the others. "At least he'll know we're back and there is nothing to report."

He connected through the operator to Cleveland and heard the phone ring at the Church. "Bishop-elect's office," Beans said with a smile in her voice.

"What is this . . . ?" Father Ellis said, fighting for words.

"Hello? Hello? Bishop-elect's office, may I help you?"

The shocked Ellis Khouri put his hand over the phone and yelled to his companions, "He's bishop-elect!"

Preparations began at once for Philip to go to Damascus for the consecration, scheduled for August 14. Passports were verified, tickets purchased, hotel reservations secured. Philip got word that Patriarch Theodosius VI would consecrate him at the Church of the Prophet Elias at the Monastery in Lebanon, just two miles from where he grew up. The bishop-elect hurriedly borrowed a set of vestments, which he would don as part of the consecration ceremony.

CONSECRATION: LEBANON

Father Philip and his entourage, including Father Paul Romley, dean of St. Nicholas Cathedral in Los Angeles, Father Lou Mahshie of St. George Church, Washington, D.C., the late Monsour Laham, vice-chairman of the archdiocese board of trustees, Rudy George, also a trustee and a lay leader from Cleveland, and the late F. K. Mittry from Los Angeles, arrived in Beirut a few days early on Wednesday, August 10. Upon his arrival Philip embraced his father and brothers in a tearful and heartwarming reunion.

For a brief time, the August storm clouds appeared to be regathering. Philip learned that the synod had not planned to give him full episcopal authority over North America, just over New York and "dependencies," that is, the outlying parishes. Such a limitation would prevent him from exercising aggressive leadership in beginning new missions and in calling American Orthodox jurisdictions to unity.

"Opposing that arrangement was one of the greatest risks he has ever taken," remembers Antoun Khouri. "He stood up to the synod before his consecration and said, 'I am going to be consecrated archbishop of New York and all North America, or else I am going to return home and report to the people that you have diminished the archdiocese in America.'

"He prevailed," said Antoun. Final preparations for the consecration took place on Saturday.

By Sunday morning, the crowd of well-wishers had grown to nearly two thousand. As the motorcade carrying the American entourage drove up the mountain toward the monastery, Philip's memories returned to another Sunday morning, in 1944—some twenty-two years earlier—when he as a boy of fourteen helped his father carry the basket of grapes to the Patriarch visiting St. Elias. This same young boy was returning home from the United States of America to become this day arch-shepherd of perhaps the greatest jurisdiction within the patriarchate of Antioch.

People had come from all over the Middle East and from all over the world. Clergy and laity, hierarchs and helpers, family and friends—hundreds came at great sacrifice to be a part of the historic celebration. Dr. Charles Malik, former president of the United Nations General Assembly, was among the special guests.

Philip and his delegation arrived at the church at nine in the morning, and the clergy immediately vested. The Divine Liturgy and the Consecration were ready to begin. Father Paul Romley, who served that day at the altar, recorded the moment in the October 1966 issue of *The Word* magazine:

Archimandrite Philip was led through the Royal Doors where he knelt before the Holy Altar. (It is noteworthy to mention the Consecration takes place after the Little Entrance of the Divine Liturgy. The Entrance into the Sanctuary typifies an entrance into heaven, and before the members of the Holy Synod take their places in the episcopal thrones—or heavenly thrones—the Consecration takes place here so the candidate may sit with them as their equal.)

The book of Holy Gospels was removed from the Altar, opened, and placed above his head. The Patriarch began reciting the prayers of Consecration. The Archbishops, who held the Gospel above the head of the candidate, in reality were holding Christ above the neck of the candidate. This was done to show that he would rule his flock after the pattern of Christ, bending his neck under the yoke of Christ, and must do nothing contrary to His will. For under the form of the Gospels, he was now taking upon his head and neck the Church of the Lord.

As His Beatitude recited the prayers of Consecration in a low and reverent voice, tears came to the eyes of practically everyone in the chapel.

METROPOLITAN PHILIP'S ADDRESS

A short time later, the new bishop was called upon to speak in response to the archpastoral charge of Patriarch Theodosius VI. Philip began:

> Your Beatitude, Brother Members of the Holy Synod, and Faithful Orthodox:
>
> With much longing, we left the New World for this good land which was blessed by the footsteps of Jesus of Nazareth. We bring to you greetings, love, and sincere obedience from your spiritual children in the United States and Canada. It is indeed a great honor for me, Your Beatitude and beloved brothers, to receive the Grace of the Holy Episcopate through the laying on of your blessed hands, which are laboring tirelessly to revive the glory of Antioch which gave Christianity thousands of saints, confessors and martyrs.

During the course of the deliberations in Damascus, between the time of his nomination on March 16, 1966, in New York and his election nearly five months later on August 5, rumors had been passed around the patriarchate that, among other things, "Philip Saliba is a sinner." On this day, giving his detractors no satisfaction, he properly admitted it!

When the Church was as pure as the light which shined on Tabor, the early Christians confessed their sins before the congregation publicly, because the sins which we commit are not against God only, but also against the community. At my priestly ordination, I confessed my sins openly and today, I confess again before God and this congregation that I have sinned more than the publican, the prodigal son, Paul, and Augustine.

From the depth of my heart, I cry like David, "Have mercy on me, O God, according to thy steadfast love, according to thy abundant mercy. Blot out my transgression. Wash me thoroughly from my iniquity and cleanse me from my sins."

Then, his remarks turned toward his view of the episcopacy and his vision for the office he had been called to occupy.

In his epistle to the Hebrews, St. Paul said, "For every high priest taken from among men is appointed for men in things pertaining to God, that he may offer both gifts and sacrifices for sins" (Heb. 5:1). The episcopate, therefore, is not a worldly, vain glory. The episcopate is first and foremost sacrifice, service, and love. The episcopate is the continuation of the eternal priesthood of Christ in time and space.

Thus, the bishop's authority is neither autocratic nor arbitrary nor absolute; it is an authority based on love and service, for "If anyone desires to be first, he shall be last of all and servant of all" (Mark 9:35). Armed with such lofty Christian principles, we launch into our pastoral work in the Archdiocese of New York and North America, an integral part of the Holy See of Antioch, the see of Peter, Paul, and Theodosius VI.

The new bishop also directed a word to the Church of Antioch. And if there was any lingering suspicion in the mind of the listener at St. Elias that he was a party to geographical sectarianism, it was dispelled here:

It is impossible for Antioch to become the bride of Christ and a hymn of praise to Him without a theological institute to breathe life in this Orthodox East where the storms of civil strife, divisiveness, doubt, and despair are blowing from all directions.

It is impossible for Antioch to recapture its past glory unless it elevates itself from the stagnant swamps of cheap politics to the esplanades of truth, goodness, and beauty. We never wanted Antioch to be Eastern or Western in the political sense. We always wanted Antioch an Orthodox Christian Church— free, independent, committed to the love of

God and neighbor, obedient to the Patriarch, the Holy Synod, and canons of ecumenical and local councils; such canons as were written by the blood of martyrs in order to enlighten and guide those who are tempted to rebel against the authority of the Church.

As he concluded his remarks, Metropolitan Philip spoke prophetically to his own future and to that of the Church at large:

We shall never bargain away the truth which liberates us from the bondage of sin. Did the Holy Fathers betray the Church when they were forced to celebrate the Eucharist in the caves and catacombs? Did the martyrs of the twentieth-century Church bargain away the truth when thousands of them went to prisons and gallows in atheistic countries? Anyone who bargains with falsehood and sells his soul to the devil will have to answer God on the day of judgment!

We promise, Your Beatitude, that we shall work with you and our venerable brothers to encourage and promote the youth movements here and in North America; for the faithful youth are the heartbeat of the Church. We assure Your Beatitude and our beloved brothers that our doors and hearts will always be open to you, and we hope that you will bless us with your visits from time to time in order to witness the discipline, faith, and progress which the archdiocese of New York and all North America has attained.

We realize that our road is long and difficult, covered with stones and thorns, full of hissing reptiles and howling wolves. But He, who has crushed the head of the serpent and calmed the sea, will raise us up when we stumble and lead us to the right path.

Elias Saliba rushed up to embrace his son after the service. It was a great day of celebration and, for many, there were tears of joy.

Monday, August 15, was the Feast of the Dormition of the Virgin Mary. In the morning, very early, Metropolitan Philip accompanied Patriarch Theodosius as they traveled from St. Elias Monastery north through the hill country to Balamand to celebrate the Divine Liturgy at the Church of the Dormition and to break ground for the new Balamand Academy. A year earlier, in 1965, Archbishop Antony Bashir had promised the patriarchate of Antioch that the archdiocese in America would build the new academy. He had fallen asleep in the Lord before he realized this dream, so his successor fulfilled the commitment on his behalf.

"I was 100 percent in agreement with Archbishop Antony's intended gift," Philip told the crowd, "because for centuries we haven't had a real Orthodox theological academy in the Middle East.

We have sent our seminarians away to study theology, in Thessalonica or Athens or in Russia—and in the early '50s some went to St. Sergios Institute in Paris. It is a great honor for me to help break ground here today for this new Balamand Seminary."

The metropolitan spent a couple of days at the school reliving his early memories from both student days and later as a teacher and dean of students. Then he went on to his first meeting as a member of the patriarchal synod.

When Philip was ready to depart Lebanon and fly to San Francisco to preside over the archdiocese convention of 1966, an airline strike had paralyzed travel to and through the major cities of Europe. He was forced to fly around the world the other way, a thirty-six-hour trip, through Manila and Honolulu on his way back to the West Coast.

"The new archbishop, seated alongside of me, was fatigued but refreshed by the thought of the challenge he was to undertake," recalled Father Paul Romley. "He was readying himself mentally for the important task which was yet to come, and I knew the voice of the Lord, which the archbishop spoke about in Beirut, echoed in his mind: 'Rise and stand on your feet; for I have appeared to you for this purpose . . .' (Acts 26:16). This was the strength given to St. Paul—the unconquerable power of truth to stand up against the dark forces of the world."

THE ARCHDIOCESAN CONVENTION:
SAN FRANCISCO

It was a physically and emotionally drained new hierarch who deplaned at the San Francisco airport. A huge delegation of clergy and laity from the archdiocese met him at the terminal, and their love and enthusiasm helped him forget his fatigue. He was about to convene the first archdiocese convention over which he would preside as metropolitan.

Philip's initial meeting with the board of trustees brought up an issue which had been brewing among the people for some time. Some members wanted to separate the administration of the archdiocese into financial matters on the one hand and spiritual matters on the other. Metropolitan Philip voiced his opposition with clarity and candor: "I object to that. There is no separation in the life of the Church between financial matters and spiritual matters. Everything in the life of the Church points to God."

Over the years a kind of dichotomy had developed. It was assumed the priest took care of spiritual things and the board or parish council looked after the finances. Those days had just come to an abrupt halt. The new metropolitan was a man in charge.

"I call that 'upstairs-downstairs theology,'" Metropolitan Philip admonished his board. "While the priest is preaching upstairs, the parish council is counting the money downstairs. This is going to stop."

Then he became more gently paternal: "Beloved, all of us must be concerned with the spiritual matters of the parish—and the arch-diocese—and all of us are committed to financial matters of the Church. Therefore, we will work together. There is no separation. The Church is not the bishop alone, nor the priest or deacon alone, nor the laity alone. The Church, from the Ortho-dox point of view, is the bishop, clergy, and people *working together*. This is the direction my episco-pate will take."

CHAPTER

6

239 85th Street

I charge you therefore
before God and the Lord
Jesus Christ, who will judge
the living and the dead at
His appearing and His
kingdom: Preach the word!
Be ready in season and out
of season. Convince, rebuke,
exhort, with all longsuffering
and teaching.

2 Timothy 4:1, 2

After the San Francisco convention the metropolitan traveled back to the Middle East to attend the sessions of the Holy Synod which were still in progress. It was another trying experience of flying halfway around the world after barely getting acclimated to Pacific Standard Time. A number of new metropolitans and bishops were elected by the synod over that summer. He stayed for some of those consecrations and then returned to his new home in Brooklyn.

A LONELY BEGINNING

It was fall 1966 when Philip walked, alone, into the empty house at 239 85th Street, Brooklyn. The place was musty, void, depressingly vacant. He had no deacon at his side, no priest to help, no secretary, nobody to cook the meals and clean the house. There was not another living soul around.

Here was the newly elected and consecrated Antiochian Orthodox Archbishop of New York and all North America all by himself in his cold, empty, dank headquarters house. "Where do I even start?" he asked himself.

At first, one of the nearby priests came over to the house to lend a hand. He helped each morning with breakfast, cleaned the kitchen, took in the volumes of mail, assisted with the correspondence and filing. And then suddenly, without warning, he left. The work load had overwhelmed him.

Next, a local deacon came to assist with the very same tasks. Eager to help, he developed a complex cycle of life: he worked three or four days with virtually no break, then slept for four days straight. "We cannot work this way," Philip finally told him. "We must set a reasonable schedule and get some discipline into our lives." The deacon nodded and walked out the door. Like the priest before him, he was gone for good.

Philip's thoughts turned toward his trusted friend Antoun Khouri, now pastor at St. George Church, Philadelphia. He reached for the telephone. "I would like you to consider moving from Philadelphia back to headquarters in Brooklyn to lend me a hand," Philip told a surprised Father Antoun.

"Wait—we are close friends," Antoun protested. "I am not sure I can work with you so soon—you are no more to me just Philip. Give me a chance, first, to adjust to you now that you are *Saidna!*" (Arabic for *Master,* the intimate name by which Orthodox people address their bishop.)

Now it was Philip who was surprised. And silent. He suspected his friend could be correct.

"But give me the chance another time," Antoun continued. "It still seems to me it's God's will for us to work together again sometime, someplace." Several months later, in 1967, Philip assigned Father Antoun to pastor St. George Church in suburban Toronto, Ontario.

Things were difficult out in the archdiocese as well. "There are a number of priests in this jurisdiction who are prepared neither theologically nor liturgically to serve in the Orthodox Church," the new primate complained to Father Alexander Schmemann one day on the telephone. "They came here without training, and I'm stuck with them. I need some good priests very badly."

The years ahead would show Philip's personal ability to select men with remarkable spiritual depth and leadership for the priesthood. "I usually know talent when I see it," he admits. His first ordination to the priesthood was Father Joseph Allen who has gone on to be pastor of St. Anthony Church, Bergenfield, New Jersey, professor of pastoral theology at St. Vladimir's and vicar-general for the archdiocese.

Besides recruiting young men in the parishes, the metropolitan never hesitated to call on men in their thirties and even their forties who were established as businessmen, to consider leaving the world of commerce to enter seminary. "What could I say but, 'Yes'?" said Father Joseph Shahda, pastor of St. George Church in Houston, when Philip asked him to leave his post as a sales executive to enroll in seminary and serve the Lord.

In the office itself many records were in disarray, virtually beyond repair. The files were nonexistent. Nobody had organized the correspondence for years, and most likely there had been precious little to file anyway. Metropolitan Antony had been a one-man headquarters: primate, custodian, and cook. In a word, he *was* the archdiocese. His sister helped him in his later years. She opened the mail, went to the bank, shopped, did laundry, handled the phone calls, and typed some of his correspondence. And for her efforts, after his death, she received the highest award given in this country by the Antiochian archdiocese: the gold medallion for service.

Historically, once a bishop is elected and consecrated to serve as a metropolitan over a national sphere, there remains one more service in the Orthodox Church which establishes his episcopal leadership: he is enthroned. This is a public service, usually held in his cathedral, and other hierarchs participate in the rite. Philip's Enthronement was held on October 13, 1966, at St. Nicholas Cathedral in Brooklyn. The primates of most of the Orthodox jurisdictions in North America were on hand, as were hundreds of the faithful from across the archdiocese, plus numerous civic leaders.

But for all that had been done in years past,

there was so much left to do. The financial systems and the annual budget were both inadequate. The clergy were often underpaid, with little retirement or insurance, and they were insecure. On some days it seemed the future of the archdiocese itself was up for discussion. Job one: to figure out where to start to make things right.

ON THE ROAD

Philip decided to start in the field, not at headquarters.

"My main concern was to know my clergy and my flock," he said looking back to those first few weeks in Brooklyn. "I embarked on a visitation program that would take me to almost every parish within the archdiocese. I found our people to be warm, hospitable, receptive to new ideas, and very eager to join hands with me to work for a brighter future for our Church."

By October of 1966 his travels had already taken him back home to Detroit, where his younger brother Najib—the one he used to pinch under the blanket—was enrolled in a Ph.D. program in history at the University of Michigan in nearby Ann Arbor. His return created quite a stir. At thirty-six, the archbishop was the youngest prelate in the entire Orthodox Church.

He arrived in town with a mustache and a stubble of a beard. "The slightness of a beard is a surprise," commented the *Detroit Free Press* in a major story in their Saturday night edition on October 22.

"I am anti-beard, and I once wrote an article against it," Philip said in the published interview. Patriarch Theodosius VI, the spiritual head of the Church in Damascus "insisted that I wear some kind of beard," Philip quipped, "and we compromised."

"Seems he feels the clergy should follow contemporary dress patterns," the reporter commented. You couldn't accuse the new metropolitan of tiptoeing around the traditional Orthodox landscape or of carefully feeling his way along in his new hierarchial post.

The next day, Sunday, October 23, 1966, the *Detroit News* took over. "Our Church has suffered for centuries from ancient and exhausted bishops," Philip was quoted as saying, "and we are now turning to younger men. You might say we have a youth movement going."

Then he beamed his remarks toward the state of American Orthodox Christianity, using as his lead comment a theme that most new bishops would probably have saved to open their tenth year in office.

"I am one of those who strongly favors a united Orthodox Church in America," he said without hesitation. "All of us already agree on all doctrines, dogmas, and traditions. We are divided into jurisdictions purely because of nationalism."

Nationalism, of course, is another name for philetism, the attitude that causes Christians to group together under the priority of ethnic identity rather than unity in Christ. It is a heresy officially condemned by the Church in the last century. "The nature of the church . . . transcends these barriers," Philip said.

He concluded the interview criticizing the use of languages like Arabic, Slavonic, and Greek in the Orthodox services in North America. "We feel that the sooner all the Orthodox Churches in America start using English, the better our chances of achieving administrative unity will be," he said.

From parish to parish he went, in each place picking up the theme of Orthodox unity in America, running the flag up the pole for just one Orthodox jurisdiction instead of many. In Altoona, Pennsylvania, in an interview in the *Mirror* on February 28, 1967, he decried the Church's inability to expand in America. Telling the truth in his customary way, he reported bluntly, "We don't have strong missionary departments."

In March he visited Austin, Texas, and called on the Roman Catholic bishop for talks. Then it was on to Tulsa, Oklahoma, where he continued on his theme of Orthodox unity in the American Church in a June 13, 1967, interview in the *Tulsa Daily World*: "The only Church which continues to cling to its native language is the Greek Orthodox. With a membership of 1.7 million in the U.S., this is by far the largest [Orthodox] group, and we need their support in breaking down the natural barriers of difference in origin."

The gauntlet for unity was laid down, and the terms were already arrestingly clear.

CONSTITUTIONAL REFORM

In 1967 the archdiocese convention was hosted by St. George of Detroit. At that conclave the metropolitan created over twenty new departments to handle areas such as sacred music, Christian education, and media relations. At the same time, he was watching over the construction of the theological academy at Balamand, for which he had sent money to finish the building project.

Then there was rewriting the constitution of the archdiocese. According to the document drafted back in 1948, only twelve people formed the archdiocese board of trustees. Philip, in view of the growth of the archdiocese under Metropolitan Antony and his own plans for calling America to Orthodoxy, believed the constitution should be changed to include far more archdiocese representation on the board. He requested and got an amendment for a forty-member board.

The archdiocese had been known as "Syrian Orthodox." The name was inherited from the days when the Church in America began as a Syrian mission to serve the Orthodox people who came from the Middle East at the turn of the century. In the meantime, many more had migrated to America from Lebanon, Palestine, Egypt, and Jordan. Because the patriarchate was named for the Church of Antioch and because Syria is a part of that Church, it made sense to the new metropolitan to broaden the title to the Antiochian Orthodox Christian Archdiocese of North America. Besides, he reasoned, for non-Orthodox Christians considering the Orthodox Faith, who would not want to be part of the Church of the apostles Peter and Paul?

With these changes in place, Philip selected an able group of lawyers and theologians to work together under his direction to rewrite the entire constitution. Presented to the convention in Miami a year later, it passed after great debate. The new constitution was put into practice in the archdiocese in 1970.

"My early years in the episcopate were the most difficult," Philip admits twenty-five years later. "I made it my business to travel to the parishes because the bishop cannot be merely the picture on the wall of the narthex. Nor can he be untouchable. He must be with his flock. Careful administration at headquarters is a plus, but you have to be out there in touch with your people."

Middle East Madness

And all these, having
obtained a good testimony
through faith, did not
receive the promise, God
having provided something
better for us, that they
should not be made perfect
apart from us.

Hebrews 11:39–40

B esides the care of the Antiochian archdiocese, a consuming burden on the heart of Philip Saliba is a workable solution to the Middle East crisis. While extremists on both sides are issuing threats and ultimatums, and with the Persian Gulf War of 1990-91 terminated, Philip believes there must be justice for both Jew and Arab in settling the dispute.

When the Arab-Israeli conflict comes up in discussion, the first question asked is often, "Who is rightful heir to the land called Palestine?"

Whether the debate concerns the year 100, 1000, 1948, 1967 or today, many Christians in the West, and even some Orthodox Christians, believe that the Jews, always and at all times, regardless of their faith in God or lack of it, hold clear title to the Holy Land. All others are usurpers. Is not Israel, after all, God's chosen people, in covenant with Him? And is it not part of His eternal plan that the regathered nation of Israel is divinely destined to be back in the Holy Land?

Further, there are some who accuse the Orthodox Church of taking an unequivocal stand on the side of the Palestinians—regardless of their tactics. Orthodox Christians reject terrorism out of hand, be it carried out by the Israelis or the Palestinians. But Orthodox believers are deeply bothered by the fact that Palestinians are being uprooted from their homes by the tens of thousands while Jewish settlers are moving in at will.

Humanitarian agencies, in reporting on Arab refugees, say most of them are being treated unjustly, and of late growing numbers of evangelical Christians and numerous Jews worldwide are expressing sober concern. And because innocent people, including small children, are paying with their lives, it is only proper for the Orthodox Church to voice its opposition to the Zionist movement in Israel.

THE BIBLE AND THE HOLY LAND

In fact, the issue is not first and foremost one of displacement and injustice, as grave as those matters are. It is a biblical issue.

The view that Israel must return physically to the land it occupied for some of its history is notably modern—which even most proponents of the view admit. Only in the twentieth century has the idea that Israel is destined to return to the Holy Land been held by more than a handful of people, and until recently, by none but a minute segment of independent protestants.

From her earliest roots in both the West and the East, the Christian Church has held firmly to an interpretation of the Bible concerning Israel that is markedly different from that of Zionism and a segment of modern evangelical protestantism. The Orthodox Church and, indeed, the great majority of Christendom holds even to this day the traditional view that the Church is the New Israel. Once this biblical perspective of the Church is understood, it becomes clear why the Orthodox Church takes the stand that it does and specifically why Philip Saliba has worked so hard for a just and fair Middle East peace.

Why is it, then, that the Orthodox Church holds the historically predominant view that Israel no longer has favored nation status as heir of destiny to the Holy Land? Four biblical truths are paramount in this consideration.

1. Palestinians Are the Native People

The ancient account of the book of Genesis in the Old Testament is clear that the Palestinians— the Philistines, as they were called—historically inhabited the Holy Land, as it came to be known. Some people are under the impression that the land belonged to the Hebrews from the very beginning. That, of course, is not the case. The Scriptures re-

veal that Abraham immigrated to Palestine from Ur
(Gen. 11:31), which is in what today is southern
Iraq near the Euphrates River. Palestine was not deserted when he arrived. It was inhabited by the Ca-
naanites (Gen. 12:6) along with the Jebusites and
the Hittites who were there some *two thousand
years* before his arrival.

Thus, when Abraham came to Palestine in
about 2000 B.C., a flourishing civilization awaited
him. The patriarchal nomad Abraham came to an
inhabited land peopled by the ancestors of the
modern Arab tribes.

This explains why, when Abraham's wife
Sarah died, he tried to secure a burial place for her
from the Palestinians (Gen. 23:1–7): "I am a for-
eigner and a sojourner among you," Abraham acknowledged to the indigenous citizens of the land.
"Give me property for a burial place among you,
that I might bury my dead out of my sight" (v. 4).

The inhabitants answered Abraham, "Hear
us, my lord: You are a mighty prince among us;
bury your dead in the choicest of our burial places.
None of us will withhold from you his burial place,
that you may bury your dead" (v. 6).

Abraham, we are told, insisted on paying
for the gravesite for Sarah. Why? It belonged to the
Palestinians, and it was their land to sell. Abraham
paid four hundred shekels of silver for the field
(Gen. 23:16).

From the start, there was an attitude of
peace between the indigenous Palestinians and

Abraham and his descendants. They are, after all, both Semitic peoples. The people therefore expressed their kindness to Abraham, offering him the best of their burial places; they even called him a prince.

Israel was eventually given the land under the old covenant, and the several peoples there were driven out because of their sin. Later, Israel was driven out because of her sin. There never was in the old covenant an unconditional promise to the land.

With this historic Old Testament record, Christians of the Middle East see no biblical justification whatever for the suffering, displacement, and death that the modern Zionists of Israel have inflicted upon them and their children.

2. The Old Covenant Has Ceased

A second reason biblically-minded Christians struggle with Israel's claim to the Holy Land is that the land was given them under the provision of what Scripture calls "the old covenant" between God and Abraham. But, to take note of a fact so obvious it is often overlooked, God has revealed that the old covenant is over!

Moreover, the old covenant was designed from the start to be temporary. It was only "a shadow of the good things to come" (Heb. 10:1), a preview to the new covenant. The book of Hebrews explains that God "has made the first [covenant] obsolete. Now what is becoming obsolete and growing old is ready to vanish away" (Heb. 8:13).

It was Jesus Christ Himself who inaugurated the new covenant, which would bring salvation not only to the Jews who believed in Him, but to Gentile believers as well. Describing this transition from the old to the new covenant, St. John wrote concerning Christ, "He came to His own [Israel], and His own did not receive Him. But as many as received Him, to them He gave the right to become children of God" (John 1:11, 12).

Thus, the old covenant and its laws were fulfilled in Jesus Christ, the incarnate Son of God. Again, the apostle John declares, "For the law was given through Moses, but grace and truth came through Jesus Christ" (John 1:17). Can the Jew be saved through Christ? Absolutely. Virtually the entire first wave of converts in the New Testament were Jews. But to find salvation, the Jew does not need to be back in the land! As Philip Saliba often quips to the press, "God is no longer in the real estate business."

A grave error in modern biblical interpretation is made by those who insist that the old covenant provisions for the nation of Israel be carried over into the new covenant. The old covenant was called an eternal covenant, but only as it is fulfilled in the light of the new covenant.

Strangely and inconsistently, those who argue that the present nation of Israel has eternal title to the land do not argue that true believers should still worship in the temple in Jerusalem, that we should sacrifice bulls, goats, or sheep for sin, or that we should keep the old covenant holy days. They recognize all this has come to its true fulfillment in the new covenant, but they doggedly and stubbornly hold out on the issue of the land. If you believe the Bible, you cannot have it both ways!

In addition, Paul the apostle clearly argues in Romans 9:8 that it is not the "children of the flesh" who are the children of God, but the "children of the promise" are regarded as descendants. And this just after he said, "They are not all Israel who are of Israel" (v. 6). The obvious biblical truth is that the current nation of Israel has nothing to do with God's true Israel. In rejecting Christ the Messiah, the modern nation keeps the conditions of neither the old nor the new covenant. Poletical Zionists are not heirs of any of God's promises.

Further in the new covenant, the earthly land is superseded by the heavenly land. The earthly Jerusalem, according to St. Paul, "is in bondage with her children" (Gal. 4:25). But the heavenly Jerusalem? "The Jerusalem above is free, which is the mother of us all" (v. 26). Those who claim the current nation of Israel is heir to the Holy Land base their claim on an outmoded covenant. It is as though they are attempting to make the modern state Israel out to be Old Testament Christians—if there were such a thing.

Worse still is that in this gross misunderstanding of the Word of God—in this modern and novel so-called "biblical interpretation"—murder, torture, rape, and persecution are justified by professing Christians! Injustice is glorified, and racism is perpetrated. It is astonishing but true that today, in the United States of America where we pledge that we believe in "liberty and justice for all," some people actually encourage Israel to seize the homes of Arabs and even kill the Palestinians and their children—and then cheer when they do so. Is this the spirit of Christ?

The Mosaic Law has passed away, the temple and sacrifices of the former worship are of no more effect, and the days of the old covenant with its provisions and promises are gone. They are fulfilled. And what is there in its place?

3. The Promises of God are for the Church

A vesperal hymn in the Orthodox Church goes, "The shadow of the law has passed by the coming of grace." In the days of old under the former covenant, the promises of God extended to His chosen people Israel. In Christ, God's promises are for all people and are lived out in the Church, His new covenant people. In Christ, there is neither Jew nor Gentile.

This is why St. Peter, himself a Jew, is so bold as to write to the early Christians, "But you are a chosen generation, a royal priesthood, a holy nation, His own special people" (1 Pet. 2:9). It is now the body of Christ, His Church who are His elect, His true priesthood, His new nation composed of both regenerate Jew and Gentile.

St. Paul, also a Jew, is just as clear. He writes to the Galatians "that the blessing of Abraham might come upon the Gentiles in Christ Jesus" (Gal. 3:14), and "if you are Christ's, then you are Abraham's seed, and heirs according to the promise" (Gal. 3:29). Because the promises of God are now for all who are joined to Christ, the Church is called "the Israel of God" (Gal. 6:16), the new Israel. The current nation of Israel is a legitimate political entity, but not heir to a covenant which has passed away.

Connected to these truths is the reality that the kingdom of God is not of this world. With the new covenant replacing the old, God's promise is no longer with one nation in one place or with one race. God's kingdom is open to all who will come, people from every nation, tongue and tribe.

4. There Must Be Justice for All

Orthodox Christians know that despite their natural tendency to side with their own flesh and blood in the Middle East conflict, there must be a just and equitable peace for all concerned.

With the presence of both Arabic and Israeli extremists, let it be repeated: it is imperative for non-Orthodox Christians to know that the Orthodox Church condemns terrorism on both sides of the border. The quarrel of Middle East Christians in that dispute is not with the existence of the nation Israel, nor is it with the historic religious tradition of Judaism, but rather with the political agenda of modern Zionism.

In 1917, at the time of the Balfour Declaration, the Jews in Palestine were an insignificant minority. The Palestinians were the overwhelming majority. "I am not saying that these two peoples should not live together," Philip is quick to point out, "but I am saying that no one people should live at the expense of the other. I believe that because of their common history, Arabs and Jews can live together. They can accommodate each other without inflicting suffering on the Palestinians— four million of whom have been unjustly displaced from their land since 1948."

A PROPOSAL

In an effort to deal with the Middle East crisis Metropolitan Philip, as early as 1968, proposed a three-point solution to the problem:

1. Creation of a Holy Land state where Christians, Muslims, and Jews will be entitled to live in peace under a democratic form of government, with the new state protected by the big powers.
2. An end to Arab belligerency and the scheme to destroy Israel.

3. Israeli willingness to allow the refugees to return home and to give up the territories occupied in the June War, as well as any plan for future expansion.

This proposal of Metropolitan Philip gained significant attention in the press, but the problem obviously still remains. At this writing, the tide of public opinion seems to be turning in favor of pressing the Israeli government to seek a peaceful solution with the Palestinians.

"The American Jewish community has become a house divided—and sometimes loudly so—over Israel's treatment of Palestinians in the occupied areas and its reluctance to pursue a comprehensive settlement that might finally bring peace to the region," writes Carl Bernstein. "A rising chorus of dissent and reassessment is being heard, even from those known for their enduring commitment to Israel" (*Time,* May 7, 1990).

Adds Philip Saliba, "My plea is that modern protestant theologians and students of Scripture take a critical and objective look at how the Church has interpreted the Bible throughout history."

THE SIX DAYS WAR

In 1967 a tragedy occurred in the Middle East. It was called the Six Days War, and the Egyptians and the Syrians suffered a humiliating defeat at the hands of Israel. Arab people were the laughingstock of the global media. The conflict resulted in the wholesale displacement of added thousands of Palestinians, and the widespread killings and sufferings had a shattering effect on the young Lebanese primate.

"I went to Washington in January 1968 to speak at the Lebanese Embassy," Philip recollects, "to get them to understand there is something we call 'public relations' in this country. It was time to take action over the poor Arab image in the United States and to tell the American people the true story about Palestinian families having been forcibly removed from their homes."

The ambassador of Lebanon hosted a dinner for Metropolitan Philip at the embassy and invited many Arab leaders in the U.S. to attend. Philip told them, "We have an ugly image in America, and we are being unjustly ridiculed. Please talk with your governments and urge them to tell the press the other side of the story."

To Philip's dismay and disappointment, one of the Arab ambassadors shouted back, "Well, go ahead and start working on it. We will help you."

"My friend," Philip said to him, "I am not a politician. That is not my job. I am here to tell you I can help you if you want my expertise in public relations and speaking to the media. But I cannot take time away from the archdiocese and vocation in the Church to become a politician!"

Philip left the dinner frustrated and very disappointed. The next day he had an appointment to visit with President Lyndon Johnson. He was warmly received in the Oval Office. Johnson, the moderately-liberal Democrat, was solidly aligned with the fundamentalist protestants in the Israel conflict. The President insisted the Arabs started the war and believed that the land was destined for Israel, no matter what. Metropolitan Philip pointed out that it was the sneak air attack by Israel against the Egyptian and the Syrian air forces that started the war. The Egyptian troops at Sinai had no air cover whatever. The battle had been decided in half an hour.

Lyndon Johnson looked squarely at Philip. "Are you telling me the Arabs didn't start the war? Why were their troops in Sinai hollering at those Jews? Why didn't they [the Arab forces] attack? Down in Texas when somebody calls you a so-and-so, you hit him right away. You don't wait for him to hit you. You take the initiative, and you hit him."

Rather than attempt a no-win answer, Philip presented the president with a beautiful Byzantine icon before he turned to leave.

"What is this?" the President asked. Lyndon Johnson thanked Philip for his visit as the primate left the White House. All the blame was still on the Arabs.

As they walked back outside, Philip asked the priest who accompanied him, "Can we ever overcome the pressure of Jewish lobbyists in Washington?"

The next day the metropolitan had an appointment at the state department. He arrived in the morning to visit with the undersecretary of state. Suddenly, he felt very weak physically, and he became dizzy. He stood up precariously and he asked to be excused.

8

Setbacks and Solutions

Those who wait
on the LORD
Shall renew their strength;
They shall mount up
with wings like eagles,
They shall run
and not be weary,
They shall walk
and not faint.

Isaiah 40:31

"I still don't know how I walked the distance to the car," Philip recalls. "The state department building is huge, and it was a long way to where we were parked. The Lord helped me make it."

He told his driver to take him immediately to the hotel. The dizziness and weakness got worse, along with a disturbing tightness in his chest. The doctor called to examine him said firmly, "We should move the metropolitan to the hospital."

HEARTSICK

That night in the hospital, Philip Saliba, age thirty-eight, suffered a mild heart attack.

Early the next morning Philip summoned Father Lou Mahshie to his bedside. "Call Father Antoun up in Toronto and ask him to come see me," he told the priest.

"When I got the call that Philip had suffered

a heart attack and was hospitalized in Washington, my first reaction was, really, that I was disgusted with myself," Antoun remembers. "I knew he had good health. I wished, then, I had said yes to help him when he asked me to come to Brooklyn back in 1966."

Antoun hurriedly packed his suitcase and took the first flight he could get, a connector from Toronto to Washington. But a heavy mist had fogged up all the major cities in the East—Boston, New York, Philadelphia—and it took him two tiresome days to reach Washington. From the airport, Antoun took a cab to Doctor's Hospital, checked with the receptionist and took an elevator up. He was overcome with both fear and fatigue.

As he walked into Philip's room, his eyes welled up at the sight of his close friend confined to bed in the cardiac ward. Then the metropolitan announced loudly, "You see, Antoun, this is all your fault! You didn't come to help me at the archdiocese." Philip's jesting was precisely what Antoun needed to halt his worry.

"Really, if you want me in the future, let me know, please," Antoun responded. "After you are back on your feet, let me know." He stayed for several days—until he was confident Philip was not in danger.

For the first two weeks, Philip did not seem to improve. The doctor confronted him one morning at his bedside. "We call what you are doing "denial." You're not making any progress because you don't believe you had a heart attack." He reviewed the medical charts with Philip and explained again what had happened.

"He was right," the metropolitan later admitted. "I refused to believe I had a heart attack. I was physically very strong. In Cleveland, I took time between five and six each evening to go to the YMCA and swim. I still played volleyball. I bragged about my physical strength. Then, suddenly, to admit I really had a heart attack—I refused to believe it."

What happened was no mystery. With the reorganization of the archdiocese, the parish visitations across the country, the pressure of the talks in Washington, he had grown weary—heartsick. He had wanted to turn the world upside down, as the Scripture says, and then right side up. But he was taking it too fast.

Wherever Philip traveled in the archdiocese, people would say, "I heard about this young archbishop—look how energetic he is. He is so young and dynamic." By his own admission he had begun to reread his own reviews and believe them.

"As I look back, the Lord was telling me something: 'Wait a minute, Philip Saliba, things are not going to happen according to your schedule. Things will happen according to My time.' I thought I was going to change history in a matter of two or three years. This heart attack was a reminder that it simply would not be so."

The experience in Washington and his recuperation in the month that followed brought about a change of direction, an altered set of priorities in Philip's life.

"Through creative suffering, I completely surrendered my life to God," he wrote of the experience. "Surrendering to God made me feel, for the first time, at peace with myself, with others, and with the world. 'Henceforth,' I said to God, 'my life belongs to You. You can do with it whatever You want.'"

At school in Lebanon, when a student misbehaves, the teacher tugs on his ear. Said Philip of his hospitalization, "I felt the Lord pull my ear."

BUILDING A TEAM

By March 1968 Philip was back at his desk. He knew it was time to begin his attack on the administrative dilemma at headquarters. Depending on a part-time deacon here or a volunteer priest there was not working. His struggle was over where to turn for help. The list of his priests was beside him on his desk. "I looked down the alphabetical list of all our clergy in the archdiocese," he recalls. "I got to the K's. There he was again, our priest in Toronto, the companion of my youth, Father Antoun Khouri. From our teen years on and through our days in seminary together, I knew him and his family to be of the highest Christian character. And very importantly, I knew he would never betray me."

Once again, Philip called Antoun on the phone. "I need you," he said, coming right to the point. "I want you to come work with me."

This time, the answer was a firm yes.

A few days later, Philip packed his bags for a trip to the West Coast to visit his parishes there. He was scheduled to serve the Palm Sunday liturgy at St. Nicholas Church in San Francisco. Father Gregory Ofiesh, the pastor, made reservations for the metropolitan at Del Webb's Townhouse where one of his parishioners, Kathy Meyer, was executive secretary.

"You need someone like Kathy to work for you at the headquarters in Brooklyn," Father Gregory told Philip on the last day of his visit. Each time the two men met in subsequent months, Father Gregory jokingly reminded Philip that he was overlooking a gold mine of competence and expertise.

A year later, Philip was back in San Francisco at St. Nicholas, and he asked Kathy Meyer to consider working for him. The youth of America had been flocking to San Francisco from all over the country, their lives a mixture of idealism and restlessness. "After watching the hippies and the flower children gather," Kathy recalls, "and listening to the sermons of Father Gregory and His Eminence about helping these young people find themselves, I decided to do something more positive with my life. I accepted the position as the metropolitan's secretary."

In July of 1969 Kathy Meyer moved to Brooklyn with all her belongings and her pet poodle, Larry. Philip's greatest fear was that when she saw the old headquarters house, she would instantly change her mind and return to the West Coast. In the tiny bedroom that had been made into an office, there was no place for her filing, just one small knee-hole desk with little or no drawer space, and a rusty manual typewriter—all this in contrast to her executive suite at Del Webb's in glittering San Francisco by the Bay.

"This is the biggest mistake I have ever made in my life!" Kathy said under her breath. Fighting back the tears on a steaming hot July afternoon the day after her arrival, she surveyed the dingy frame headquarters house in Brooklyn. "This place is a wreck!" She arrived just as Metropolitan Philip was leaving for the convention in Miami. After one look around, she gave serious thought to boarding a plane back to San Francisco.

"But there was a man, Edmund Saleeby, who helped me get settled in a neighborhood nearby. He drove me around to find furniture, he introduced me to his friends and family, and he made me feel welcome. If it hadn't been for him, I'd honestly have gone back home before the archbishop returned from Florida."

Sometime after Kathy Meyer settled in, a personality conflict developed between visiting Lebanese Bishop Elia and Larry, her fourteen-year-old dog. On the days Larry went to the groomer, he accompanied her to the office, and invariably these were the days the bishop came by. Larry typically raised his lip and greeted the bishop with a menacing growl. There was strong mutual disdain, and the tension between the two continued to build. The bishop could never understand why the dog was incessantly bathed, clipped, and manicured— and why he wore a jeweled collar and a ribbon.

Then, unexpectedly, Larry became terminally ill. Kathy had no choice but to take him on a final, one-way journey to the veterinarian's office. A week later, Bishop Elia stopped by the office. "Where is Larry this morning?" he asked of his canine nemesis.

"I had to have him put to sleep," Kathy answered in a somber tone.

"Put to sleep!" the Bishop repeated with a chuckle which soon erupted into steady laughter. Missing the idiom, the Lebanese native could not figure out what a sleeping dog had to do with his question. Kathy, on the other hand, presumed his hilarity to be a cruel, vindictive judgment on the animal he loved to hate. Philip claims it was at least a month before she resumed speaking to the bishop. Twenty years later the story is still told at convention banquets to the delight of the crowd.

Today, Kathy Meyer is the "right hand" of the archbishop and the archdiocese. She has carved her niche of irreplaceability over nearly twenty-two

years. And she loves her job. "I feel I am doing
some good," she says, "and I know it is good for me
spiritually."

Part of her role is that of protector. "Over
the years I have learned what to bother him with
and what not to bother him with. People call and
say, 'I've got to talk with the archbishop right
away!' And ninety-nine times out of one hundred,
it's something that can wait."

THE CHILDREN

From the start, Philip built lasting friendships with the children. Whenever he visits a parish, he makes it a point to speak with the children
as a group and hold the youngest in his arms. The
word got around that he would answer their letters, and soon floods of short, handwritten notes
came to him from his youthful devotees around the
country. Many were absolutely disarming:

Dear Sayidna,
I read your Christmas Meditation and I en-
joyed it. I just had to write and tell you how
good it was. I didn't think you wrote it at first.
I hope you had a Merry Christmas and a
Happy New Year.
                            Love, Loretta

Dear Metropolitin Phillip,
Hi! Im gonna miss you while your gone. But, I

was thinking, how fun it would be if we changed places. So, this poem is for you. On my topic, "changing places." It's called "wondering." Enjoy!

> Wondering
> I know what I feel like
> But Id like to be you,
> and feel like you feel like
> and do what you do.
> Id like to change places
> for maybe a week,
> and look like you look,
> and speak as you speak.
> and think what you think,
> and go where you go,
> and feel what youre feeling
> and know what you know.
> I wish we could do it,
> change from head to toe,
> always choosing right,
> always friend, not foe.
> oh what fun it would be,
> If I could be you once,
> and you could be me!
>
> Love, Marina

Dear Metropolitan,
Keep on Bishopin!
Your *my* kind of Bishop

> Love, Mark

Some of the letters were almost entirely made up of questions, and what queries they were!

Dear Arch-bishop,
How old are you? What do you like about school? Do you like church? Is your job hard? Do you like sports? Was your father an arch-bishop? Do you sleep with your hat? How many times do you pray every day? Do you watch basketball games, football games and baseball games? What time do you go to bed? Where do you live? Did you ever go to Syria, Europe, or Germany. Do you like to brush your teeth? Did you ever get grounded? Did you ever see god in your dreams? I'm 10 and I'm in the 5th grace.

Sincerely, Camille

The Arabic word for uncle is *Amou,* but Philip's young niece could only say "Meemoo" when she learned to talk. The name stuck, and this is her thank-you note for a ring he sent her.

Thank you, Meemoo, for the beautiful ring,
I don't know anyone who could possess such
 a gorgeous thing.
I love you very much as you may already
 know,
The ring is as beautiful as fluttering snow,
The ring sparkles in the sunlight,
It's sometimes hard to look at because its so
 bright

I love you right Now and I'll love you
   forever,
And I'll wear this ring on Christmas in
   December.
>   From Leslie Saliba

For years, the Metropolitan received a box every few months along with a short note from the "Cookie Girl."

Dear Sayedna,
I really haven't seen you in such a long time. I miss you very, very much. I made a batch of chocolate chip cookies. They are homemade. i really hope you like them. Well, there is nothing else to say but, I LOVE YOU.
>   Love, Alison
>   (Your Cookie Girl)

One day, the most curious of all the cards and letters arrived. The text was strange, and the name was unfamiliar.

Hi.
   I'll say it again and again and again. . . .
You're WONDERFUL—Honest
>   Omar
P.S.
   You have a bigger pull in heaven than me. Please pray for me. I am sick and my mommy took me to the Drs. twice, the first time I thought it was curtain time. It's very discom-

fortable, making my hair fall out on my face
and legs.

So dear Archbishop, Most Reverend Met,
please pray for this old dog who loves you
dearly.

The last sentence cleared up the mystery at the second reading. Omar was a bulldog.

Gradually things began taking shape in the
office. Father Antoun Khouri had assumed a significant part of the load. Kathy was a Godsend; the
boss-secretary chemistry was exactly right. The
new administration was solidly in place. Philip
knew the Lord had answered his prayers.

Beyond Brooklyn, the priests out in the parishes were at peace. They had a shepherd whose
voice they knew, and he knew them. Letters and
calls were up to date. There were fewer frustrations
and complaints.

No longer at the mercy of his schedule and
public demands, the new archbishop was becoming a man in control. Like St. Paul, he was im-
mersed in the apostolic ministry with "the care of
all the churches," enthusiastic about his charge,
and preaching the Word of God with boldness.

9

New Heart,
New Home

Unless the LORD
builds the house,
They labor in vain
who build it.

Psalm 127:1

The home in Brooklyn, which had been the headquarters of the archdiocese and the bishop's residence for years, was getting old and rickety. And it was too small. Now that records were being kept systematically, there was little space left over for books and office work. Philip was planning to hire another secretary to help with the expanding workload, which would mean giving up the space set aside for house guests—bishops on visits from the old country and priests in town for meetings. The Brooklyn house had become obsolete both for the current operation of the archdiocese and for Philip's vision for the future.

The dreamer began to dream.

Together with his lay leaders, Philip looked first in Brooklyn but could not find anything suitable. They decided to be bold and consider moving across the Hudson. At first they looked for open land on which to build. In that process they discovered a large home for sale in Englewood, New Jersey. Antoun Khouri and Philip walked through the house and liked it very much. It was spacious and in a prime location, a beautiful residential neighborhood just five minutes from the George Washington Bridge and fifteen minutes out of downtown Manhattan. The residence itself was surrounded by 3.5 acres of land, and behind the main house stood a two-story frame guest house. They asked about the price and were told the owners wanted $200,000. They were able to settle on $175,000. They moved across the river in 1971. "We were extremely fortunate to find this beautiful property with the amount of land which we have—and the trees," Philip said.

And then he opened his soul. "I love trees. I feel many times, especially in the spring, summer, and fall, that the trees absolutely hug this house with tenderness and love. In the autumn I watch the leaves coming down, and it's a reminder of life itself in its natural cycle. This seasonal change is something we never fully experienced in Brooklyn because of the density of the population and the homes so closely built.

"And when it snows, you look outside. Across the yard you see those same beautiful trees, now barren, with all this snow on them. Sometimes in Brooklyn I used to think the snow was black. But here you see it is pure white."

Besides the abundant extra room for office space and guest quarters, two other rooms were added. There is the Chapel of St. John Chrysostom just across the hallway from the metropolitan's office, a wonderful, quiet refuge for prayer. Then, at the back, a spacious dining room—actually a small banquet hall—was added for large dinner meetings and receptions. This room has held numerous historic meetings with patriarchs, heads of state, governors, and ambassadors. It has also been the setting of dialogues with groups of people from other Christian bodies who have come to seek out the Orthodox Church.

A SPIRITUAL HOUSE

In the Old Testament, once the house was built the Spirit of the Lord came to fill it. Philip sensed a similar pattern was appropriate for the archdiocese itself. The visible part of the structure was set: the office, the finances, departmental reorganization, and now the new headquarters and residence.

It was time to tackle the spiritual needs. He decided to speak out more aggressively against the social evils of the day. Then there was the matter of new missions. And he wanted to meet the spiritual needs of Orthodox youth, both in his own archdiocese and throughout North America.

Internally, the Antiochian Orthodox people on the American continent were still split into the two factions, centered in New York and Toledo. That schism, dating back to 1936, was yet to be healed. The other division, the external one, was

fifteenfold in nature—the fifteen Orthodox jurisdictions in North America operating independently of each other. Philip was committed to
solving the internal problem first, but he was determined to work on both of them together.

In an interview with the Louisville, Kentucky, *Record* July 24, 1975, Philip stressed that
the movement toward Orthodox unity in America
is "inevitable because we already have the unity of
faith." From the very start of his episcopacy he had
been anticipating the day when there would be one
jurisdiction, not fifteen. "We're not a Church of
immigration anymore," he told the reporter. "The
ethnic spirit which permeated the pioneers has dis-
appeared."

In 1973 the Supreme Court issued its famous 5-4 decision known as *Roe v. Wade,* which
legalized abortion in the United States. Philip Saliba did not budge an inch from the stance Orthodox Christians had taken throughout history.

A story in the Atlanta *Journal,* August 22,
1973, summarized his beliefs. "In our moral theology, willful abortion is equated with murder,"
Philip said. The Supreme Court decision in his eyes
changed absolutely nothing. "What is legal is not
necessarily moral," he explained. For Orthodox believers, the state does not supersede the Church.

Another issue bringing widespread disrup-
tion to protestant denominations in the 1970s was
women's ordination. Significantly, at the 1973 convention of the Antiochian Orthodox Church in At-

lanta, the women themselves instigated and passed a resolution that the matter of women's ordination not even be considered by the convention delegates.

"Women have always played a central role in the Orthodox Church," Philip has said repeatedly. "And though in the New Testament and Church history there is no tradition of women in the priesthood or the episcopacy, I am for bringing back the office of deaconess in the Church." Traditionally women have served as Orthodox deacons—helping with the sick, the homeless, the downtrodden—but not in recent years.

The year 1975 marked a watershed in the charismatic movement in America. Predictably balanced in his assessment of the phenomenon, Philip commented in the same interview, "We [in the Orthodox Church] don't need a new theology of the Holy Spirit. Renewal, yes, but not a new theology." He went on to assert that the Orthodox Church was already charismatic in its theology, a statement that baffles many modern pentecostal Christians who feel that liturgy and sacrament stifle the work of the Holy Spirit. Interestingly, many of the convert clergy in the Antiochian Orthodox Archdiocese came out of the charismatic renewal of the 1970s and 1980s.

SOYO

SOYO had originally stood for the Syrian Orthodox Youth Organization. When the name of the archdiocese changed in 1969 to Antiochian Orthodox, the call letters of SOYO stayed the same. But the title became the Society of Orthodox Youth Organizations.

This youth movement, SOYO, was born on the battlefields of World War II. It was started under Metropolitan Antony Bashir. Father Ellis Khouri had been one of the prime movers in its establishment. The war had served to alert the youth to the brevity and uncertainty of life. After witnessing atrocities overseas firsthand, the incredible suffering and death, those who served in the armed forces came home with the realization that God must control their destiny and their lives.

At first, SOYO was organized to supply teachers for parish education and to bolster parish choirs. Soon the organization began to sponsor charitable efforts to help the poor and the hungry. From those active in the late 1940s and the 1950s came a number of outstanding Orthodox priests who serve the Church today.

Having traveled across North America early in his episcopacy, Philip had found ample opportunity to examine the progress of SOYO, and he determined that improvement was needed. "By the late '60s, our Orthodox youth had become spiritually stagnant," he said. He decided on two moves toward improvement.

First, Philip formed a new branch of SOYO—Teen SOYO—to provide a home in the Church for the soon-to-be adults. Helen Rihbany of Boston was asked by the metropolitan to lead the group, and she chaired the first national meeting of the organization in August 1968 at the archdiocesan convention in Pittsburgh. The first elected Teen SOYO president was Bobby Laham, also of Boston, who led the movement with dedication and hard work. Minutes of that first conclave show that from the start Teen SOYO was involved with sponsoring spiritual retreats, raising money for the poor, and providing social activities for the youth.

Next, at the 1970 archdiocesan convention in Chicago, the metropolitan called a meeting. "You have become basically a social organization," Philip told the SOYO delegates. "We drink a lot of coffee together, but there's not much substance or spiritual depth." The delegates agreed.

"Therefore, we must add two important principles to the SOYO movement: first, an awareness of who we are and, second, a specific commitment of ourselves to Christ and the Church.

"Regarding awareness, we cannot know who we are without some study. I am calling on you to begin reading the Holy Scriptures along with the writings of the early Church fathers. Once we have some self-awareness, then we are ready to make a new commitment to really being Orthodox Christians."

Philip had laid down the challenge, and rejuvenation seemed to set in at once. But the progress went a step further. The SOYO conventions of the past included only the youth. Now the realization came that the Church is everyone, the whole Christian community, not just the young. So the SOYO conventions took a dramatic shift. They became regional Parish Life Conferences—six of them each summer—and entire families attended. SOYO had its meetings, as did the Christian Education Department, the Liturgical Commission, and all the rest. The crowds jumped from scores of people to hundreds.

"The Parish Life Conferences have added a new dimension to the spiritual life of the archdiocese," Philip observes. "There is nothing to match parents and children praying together, young and old alike in Bible study groups and interaction."

THE DEDICATION AT BALAMAND

The year 1971 again saw Philip back at Balamand for the dedication of the seminary for which he had raised the needed funds and broken ground a few years earlier. Through the generosity of the Antiochian lay people in America, the project was seen through to glorious completion.

With the death of Patriarch Theodosius VI in 1970, Elias IV was elected, and he presided over the dedication ceremonies. The man who would later be Patriarch Ignatius IV was then a bishop, serving as dean of the school. Philip had been asked to speak to the crowd, which had come from all over Lebanon.

"For us in the Church of Antioch, it is not enough to build this school out of these rugged, beautiful stones," he began. "Now we invite the all-Holy Spirit to breathe life into the school, to create by His grace a spiritual atmosphere here.

"Further, we must do more than train our young Syrian and Lebanese Christians through the study of theology. Along with that, I am calling on you, the laity of the Church, to support your parishes with your generous financial gifts so that Orthodox Christianity will continue to have a future here in the Middle East."

Traditionally, the parish priests in Syria and Lebanon held jobs outside the Church to provide for their wives and children. Often they taught school. In the larger cities, some priests were supported by the Church, but in the villages where the people were often poor, there was no built-in contribution program to support the priest.

"We have built a school to educate our future leaders," he continued, "but my concern is that if we don't devise a way to financially provide for leaders in our parishes, those who come here to study theology will have no place to use their training."

The dedication of the seminary became a landmark event not only in Lebanon, but in the ongoing history of the Antiochian Orthodox Christians in North America. Arabic Christians in North America sense, of course, a particular kindred spirit and attachment to the people in the

Middle East, for most were born of parents who came to America at the turn of the century from Lebanon, Syria, Palestine, Egypt, and Jordan. The building of the school served to remind the American faithful that the Church is the Church whether it is in Lebanon or Russia or North Africa. Their financial participation gave them a way to return a tangible thank offering to God and to their fellow Christians in the Old World.

TRAINING AMERICAN CLERGY

Back home, Philip continued to work for excellence in the archdiocese. A primary concern had been improved theological education for his future priests. He was candid with his trustees when he returned from Damascus: "Frankly, the money we have budgeted for theological education is insignificant. We must set a new goal—to underwrite the education of our future clergy in this archdiocese." Plans were drawn to invite both parishes and individuals to contribute directly to the training of future priests and parish workers.

In addition, a new policy was enacted in the archdiocese: henceforth, no priest would be ordained unless he was a graduate of an accredited college and an Orthodox seminary. The one exception would be seminary-trained pastors of non-Orthodox Christian bodies who, with their people, came to be part of the Antiochian Orthodox Archdiocese. With supplemental training available, they would be received on a case-by-case basis.

Father Joseph Allen thinks back over his own experience: "The day I graduated from St. Vladimir's, he started pushing me to start on my doctorate. He wanted from the beginning to make theological education normative for us as priests. It is at his insistence that we have programs in homiletics and pastoral theology at the seminary today. And to supplement this training he began the St. Stephen's Correspondence Course."

"Today, when I look at the quality of the priests we have, I say, 'Thank God that this struggle with theological education has been won!'" Philip told his trustees in the mid 1980s. "It has led us from the wilderness of ignorance and doubt to the promised land of deep Christian commitment and great spiritual achievement on the part of the priests in our archdiocese today."

HEART REPAIR

Philip had navigated through life more carefully since his heart attack in 1968. But in 1972, at the Los Angeles convention, he felt that tightness in his chest again. One evening he could not walk from his hotel across the street to a restaurant. The pain was staggering. "I must do something about this," he told Father Antoun. "It's not fair to the archdiocese; it's not even fair to me."

By mid-September, with the SOYO conferences and the L.A. convention behind him, it was time to take action, to make the decision to have the problem repaired. He spent a few evenings alone at his residence trying to determine the best route to take. The passage in Jeremiah 30:17 came to Philip's mind: "For I will restore health to you, And heal you of your wounds," says the LORD.

Open heart surgery was in its primitive stages in those days. Over the years Philip had met some outstanding specialists in Los Angeles, in San Francisco, and at the Cleveland Clinic in Ohio. "I went through a difficult period trying to decide not when the operation should be but where. Then I thought back to a brilliant young cardiologist who was doing his internship in Cleveland when I was a priest there. His name was Dr. Eugene Sayfie."

By 1972 Dr. Sayfie had moved to the Miami Heart Institute. Philip called him and explained the problem. "I believe I need open heart surgery."

"Well, you come down and we will give you a catheterization and have a look inside."

Philip had already had a catheterization in San Francisco and one in Cleveland. So he back-pedaled. "Can't you get the pictures from San Francisco or from Cleveland?" he asked the doctor.

"Oh, no. We are going to take our own pictures so everything's up to date."

They did, and the diagnosis was clear: the operation was needed. Surgery was scheduled for Monday, September 8, 1972.

"Many times when I have difficulties or

problems, I leave my desk and go to the chapel across the hall and pray," Philip says. "I come back refreshed. So I went to the chapel right before leaving the house to fly to Miami, and I knelt in front of the altar. I prayed, 'God, if it is Your will to continue my work in this archdiocese, I pray that You will guide the physician's hands and restore me to health.'"

Accompanying the metropolitan on the flight to Miami were Father Antoun, Philip's youngest brother Najib, and Najib's wife Elaine. A young receptionist at the Heart Institute greeted them, and Philip was asked to step over to an office where the admittance nurse would ask him some questions.

"Hi, my name's Jenny," the nurse said. "And you are Mr. . . . ?"

". . . Saliba," Philip said, wondering to himself why, when he was in a clerical collar and a black suit, he would be greeted as "Mister." Perhaps she was unfamiliar with Christianity in its historic tradition, he reasoned.

"Please have a seat right over here," Jenny said, motioning him to a green metal-frame chair beside her desk. "Let's start by having you give me your full name."

"All right," Philip said. "It is Archbishop. . . ."

"Wait," she interrupted with a smile, "that's an unusually long first name. Let's see, that's A-R-C-H-B—can you help me with that?"

Philip had to spell the title for her twice and

then go through the rest of his name with her, explaining briefly what an archbishop or a metropolitan does in the Orthodox Church.

"That's great," she said mechanically, moving quickly on to the next question. "What is your wife's name?"

Again, a brief explanation on the celibate life of the bishop was in order.

"The number of your children, and their names?" Jenny asked without missing a beat.

After twenty minutes of consternation, Philip thanked the nurse and was shown to his room. He was informed that surgery was scheduled first thing in the morning. Father Antoun and Najib helped him get settled.

That evening Philip asked that Father Michael Husson, the priest at St. George Cathedral in nearby Coral Gables, come and serve him communion. The doctor had ordered Philip a sleeping pill, but he refused it. He preferred instead to surrender himself to the Lord's care and comfort. Before turning out the light he asked that Father Antoun pray for him, and read to him his favorite Psalm, Psalm 51. The two men recited the Psalm together from memory, the prayer of David's confession.

> Have mercy upon me, O God,
> According to Your lovingkindness;
> According to the multitude of Your
> tender mercies,
> Blot out my transgressions.

Wash me thoroughly from my
iniquity,
And cleanse me from my sin.
(vv. 1–2)

Philip fell soundly asleep in peace.

SURGERY

"Are you ready for the operation?" a nurse asked a still dozing Philip just after daybreak.

"I am ready," he said.

The operation lasted six hours. Dr. Eugene Sayfie was there to oversee the surgery, alongside the heart surgeon and the anesthesiologist.

Philip regained consciousness in the recovery room. The nurse was nearby. "I feel like a space man, with all these tubes coming out of me," he said to her, dazed.

Then he remembered a very strange experience that occurred while he was unconscious. "I don't know how to explain it. I found myself in a beautiful place. There were flowers, green trees, water. It was like God had given me a glimpse of paradise."

After recuperating in the hospital, Philip was released on October 14 and was driven to Fort Lauderdale to move into the apartment of close friends in the archdiocese, George and Elaine Karam. They had donated their oceanside residence to the metropolitan for further rest. Father Antoun stayed there with him.

"I remember vividly the first time I walked out on the beach. I felt I wanted to bless every grain of sand. It was like being born again! I went out into the water, and while it was too soon for me to swim, I felt like hugging every wave in that peaceful ocean. The Lord was so good to me, allowing me to continue to serve Him in our beloved archdiocese."

After two months of rest, Philip packed his bags and returned home to Englewood to resume his work and to dream again his dreams.

CHAPTER

10

Three Dreams Fulfilled

When the righteous
are in authority,
the people rejoice.

Proverbs 29:2

Thanksgiving Day and the Advent season of 1972 found Philip Saliba home in Englewood, grateful and rejoicing. He felt, literally, like a new man with a new heart. And with the new year at hand, he decided to sit down and map out his goals.

ANTIOCHIAN WOMEN

His priority for 1973 would be to organize a national Orthodox women's movement in the archdiocese. He would begin by calling together a group of his most faithful women for a preliminary session.

"Whatever parish I visit, I find the most active people in the parish are you ladies," he told a group of women at the initial meeting in early 1973. "You are teaching in our Sunday schools, singing in our choirs, serving in the kitchens, and keeping the parish offices afloat. I know that if you can do all this and more on the parochial level, you can certainly do an excellent job on the national level as well. With so many people in this world we have to reach with the gospel, with our many projects designed to help those in need, who can do a better job of leadership in these matters than you Orthodox Christian women?

"You read the Scriptures, and you find so many good women in the Old and New Testaments who are more faithful to God than the men! I always think of how at the cross, for example, all of the disciples deserted our Lord Jesus Christ except one group. Who was it that stayed there with Him? A group of devoted women! They were there to share in His sufferings."

Predictably, the women of the archdiocese responded with great enthusiasm. The Antiochian Orthodox Christian Women of North America (AOCWNA) was born that day. The metropolitan appointed a commission of officers headed by Pauline Maloof of St. Anthony's Church, Bergenfield, New Jersey, as the first president. Father John Badeen, now pastor of St. Michael Church, Beaumont, Texas, put his legal mind to work and assisted as they drafted the constitution. The following year, with the constitution in place, Philip called the Antiochian women together to elect officers. "Now it is your job to choose the new slate of officers for your organization." They elected the same people Philip had appointed to serve a year earlier.

Since the founding of the AOCWNA organization, the women have never disappointed their primate. When he informed them in 1987 that St. George Hospital in Beirut was in desperate need of funds, they raised nearly $200,000, enabling hundreds of war-torn Lebanese people—Christians and non-Christians—to receive medical care. They have contributed hundreds of thousands of dollars to the needy and the poor, as well as to special archdiocesan projects such as summer camp programs and the campus ministry.

A TIME FOR HEALING

From the very day of his enthronement as archbishop of New York and all North America, Philip's dream was to re-unify the Antiochian Orthodox Christians on the continent. For the Orthodox Christians in America under the patriarchate of Antioch had been divided into two separate bodies for decades. This schism and its healing serve both as an example of Philip's God-given commitment to work effectively for unity, and as an inspiration to others with a passion to knit splintered Christian factions back together.

The first bishop of any national background ever consecrated on American soil was of Arabic heritage, a son of Antioch named Raphael Hawaweeny. His consecration was overseen by Bishop Tikhon, now a saint of the Church, who had presided over all the Orthodox faithful in America, be they Russian, Greek, Arabic, or other ethnic identity. Bishop Tikhon was in America under the patriarchate of Moscow.

The new Bishop Raphael was placed in charge of the Syrian-Arabic mission of the Russian diocese. Though ultimately the Greek Orthodox Church gained a primate, as did the Serbians and certain other jurisdictions, the Antiochian parishes remained united under Bishop Raphael.

When Bishop Raphael died in 1915, however, Antiochian Orthodox Christians began to divide. Their allegiance was split between those who were loyal to the patriarchate of Moscow, under which Bishop Raphael had been consecrated, and those loyal to the patriarchate of Antioch, which oversaw the Church in their homelands. This Russian-Antiochian schism was in many ways an extension of old tribal conflicts among the Arabic immigrants to North America, and the division became a growing disgrace to the Church.

In the absence of singular leadership, the bitterness between the two groups increased, sometimes even resulting in civil lawsuits over the ownership of Church property. Instead of the synod of Moscow (which was by now hampered in its effectiveness because of the Bolshevik Revolution of 1917) and the synod in Antioch trying to work out a solution, the people in the U.S. and Canada were left to themselves to deal with the division. The problem only grew worse. This humiliation continued on into the mid 1930s.

Finally, in 1936 the new Patriarch of Antioch, Alexander III, dispatched one of his metropolitans, Theodosius, to America to assess the situation and determine the consensus of the people in an effort to establish a new bishop and thereby unify the two factions. (This same Metropolitan Theodosius went on to become Patriarch Theodosius VI in 1958.)

Church records indicate that Archimandrite Antony Bashir received the overwhelming majority of the votes of the clergy and laity to become the new Antiochian Orthodox bishop in North America. Antony was very gifted in both Arabic and English and was a dynamic shepherd. He seemed to be the one who could serve to bring the archdiocese fully into the twentieth century.

He had been opposed in the nomination process by Samuel David, who resided in Toledo, Ohio. Though not as well acclimated to American culture as Antony, he was a good and humble man at heart and a tireless worker in the Church. There was a strong, vocal minority of people who had favored Samuel David in the election, many of these having come from the villages of Lebanon near the place where he had grown up. This faction, though greatly outnumbered in the voting, was unwilling to accept the election of Antony Bashir.

Thus on the same day Antony Bashir was being consecrated archbishop of New York, April 16, 1936, another consecration took place. The followers of Samuel David had convinced two Russian bishops to come to Toledo to consecrate their candidate as the archbishop of Toledo. The Russian-Antiochian schism had evolved into a new American conflict between the archbishops of Toledo and New York.

With both primates, technically at least, under the patriarch of Antioch the tensions were gradually exported back to Damascus. Soon parties from both archdioceses were making trips back to Syria in an effort to secure the upper hand of power. The civil suits over property continued, and money and effort were spent needlessly while each side guarded its turf. It was the carnality and factionalism of ancient Corinth all over again, now transported to the soil of Orthodox America.

By the time Philip came to Boston in 1956, the problem had escalated and spread to many of the major cities in the U.S. and Canada, where there were often two competing Antiochian parishes—one under Toledo, the other under New York. Cousins were not speaking to cousins; neighbors and life-long friends shunned each other at the marketplace and on the street corner. Christians behaved like nonbelievers.

"This makes no sense at all," Philip told Emile Hanna as they both switched from Toledo to New York in the days following their study at Holy Cross. "Why should we even have to make such a choice?"

By the time Philip assumed primacy in the Archdiocese of New York in 1966, he was firmly committed to study the situation and prepare for the day he would make his move toward solving the split. Frankly assessing the problem with his trustees in 1970, he said, "If we believe in Orthodox unity in North America, then our unity must begin with ourselves. Before we can talk of alignment with our Greek, Russian, and Romanian brothers, we must bring our own people together as one."

In 1962, four years after the death of Samuel David, Michael Shaheen had been consecrated bishop of Toledo. He and Philip saw each other at meetings of the Holy Synod in Damascus, but had no contact at all back home. While there was no outward personal animosity between the two leaders, there was no communication between them either.

A MOVE TOWARD REUNION

In 1973, a SOYO (Society of Orthodox Youth Organizations, the youth movement of the New York archdiocese) convention was being held in Toledo, the see of Archbishop Michael Shaheen. Metropolitan Philip was present there with his people and many of the priests of his archdiocese, including Father George Rados, then of St. George Church in Terre Haute, Indiana. The convention had concluded with the Divine Liturgy on a bright, sunny Sunday, June 24. Father George was visiting over coffee with the metropolitan in his suite after the service.

Philip looked up at Father George during a lull in the conversation. "I've got an idea," the metropolitan said to his priest. "Go to the phone and call Archbishop Michael."

"Do you mean it?" asked Father George, not making a move, thinking privately he was being set up as the butt of a prank. "Do you really want to see him?"

"I want to visit him, yes. I'm telling you to get up and call the man," Philip said with a taunting grin.

Father George placed the call and announced to the archbishop that he and the metropolitan would like to pay an afternoon visit.

"You're welcome to come by," Archbishop Michael said.

The two men took the hotel elevator down to the garage level, got in the car, and drove across the city to the archbishop's residence. They parked, walked up to the front door, and knocked.

Archbishop Michael came to the door. The eyes of the two prelates met, and at Michael's invitation Philip stepped inside and embraced his distant friend. "We have come to talk about unity," he announced to Michael.

They moved through the entrance hall into the living room and sat down.

"I can't understand why we are divided," Philip began. "We should unite our people together, you and I. If it is your desire to be the metropolitan, so be it. If you want me to be the metropolitan, I will be happy to serve. Just tell me what you would prefer, and we will do it."

Archbishop Michael was most receptive to the unexpected overture. "Yes," he said, "let us begin to work on it."

Their mutual decision that day was to appoint a commission to meet and study the options for bringing the two groups together. The commission, composed of Archpriest John Estephan for Toledo and Fathers George S. Corey and George M. Rados for New York, would set down a list of principles to guide the merger. Philip's aim: one united Antiochian archdiocese of North America, one metropolitan primate, and one auxiliary archbishop, one vote in the synod of Antioch, one youth movement, and common finances. Each party would present these guidelines to its constituency.

As with most attempts at unity, progress was spotty at first. On the plus side, Philip was very warmly received at St. George of Charleston, West Virginia, a parish under Toledo the following September, 1973. He spoke to an overflow crowd of six hundred at their annual Labor Day Banquet, and the response at the mention of unity was most enthusiastic.

On the strength of the enthusiasm of that event, Philip asked for a summit meeting involving the leadership of both archdioceses to be held in Pittsburgh later in the fall. By contrast, that meeting did not go well, with both sides dwelling on the negatives of the past. And a second such summit meeting in early 1974 was fruitless as well. But both sides agreed to keep talking, believing that the next meeting should involve the two primates.

On March 25, 1974, the two archbishops and others from each archdiocese met in Englewood, New Jersey. They came to agreement on a number of items in the original agenda. Negotiations became deadlocked, however, over the issue that one hierarch, not two, would be part of the Holy Synod of Antioch. With that obstacle standing in the way of unity, talks were suspended.

But on June 24, 1975, the two archbishops met again in Pittsburgh at St. George Church in the office of Father George S. Corey and reached a point of reconciliation. They signed the agreement drafted by the commission, reuniting the Antiochian Orthodox Christians of North America.

THE AGREEMENT

The key points of the agreement included the following:

- There shall be one, united Antiochian Archdiocese to be called, "The Antiochian Orthodox Christian Archdiocese of North America."
- The Primate of this one, united Antiochian Archdiocese will be Philip Saliba, with the title "Metropolitan." The Auxiliary of

this one, united Antiochian Archdiocese will be Michael Shaheen, with the title, "Archbishop."

• This one, united Antiochian Archdiocese will have one vote in the Holy Synod of Antioch. Both the Metropolitan and the Archbishop have the right to participate in the Synod meetings. In the absence of the Metropolitan, the Archbishop has the right to vote in behalf of the Metropolitan.

• The Metropolitan will reside at the archdiocesan headquarters in Englewood, New Jersey. The Archbishop will reside at the archdiocesan headquarters in Toledo, Ohio.

• The Metropolitan shall be commemorated in all liturgical services of the churches of the one, united Antiochian Archdiocese, as defined by canon law. The Archbishop shall commemorate the Patriarch and the Metropolitan in all divine services.

• This one, united Antiochian Archdiocese in North America will have one treasury, one Board of Trustees, one youth organization, one program for theological students, one religious education and sacred music program, the same discipline for clergy, laity and parishes, the same insurance program for the clergy and the same youth Parish Life and Archdiocesan conferences and conventions. In short, we will be one in every respect in reference to the Antiochian faithful in North America.

That summer, there was great rejoicing among all the people at the Antiochian archdiocesan convention held in Louisville, Kentucky. Archbishop Michael was received with enthusiastic warmth, amid a veritable explosion of joy and Christian love at the July conclave.

REFERRAL TO THE HOLY SYNOD

On August 19 both archbishops attended the session of the Holy Synod at St. Elias Monastery in Lebanon. The two men announced with excitement and expectation, "The Antiochian faithful are united in North America!" The signed agreement was submitted to the synod for its consideration and ratification.

"Who gave you permission to do this?" sneered one of the bishops. Philip was dismayed. But he never had a chance to answer. Patriarch Elias, with all his spontaneity and outspokenness, jumped to his feet. He looked his brother bishop squarely in the eyes.

"I don't understand you!" the Patriarch screamed at the top of his voice. "Aren't you ashamed of yourself! When you should be presenting these men with bouquets of roses, congratulating them, decorating them for their valor in uniting the people after sixty years of strife and division—and you want to give them *permission* to unite?"

The detractor slumped down in his chair. There was nothing more for him to say. Everyone signed the agreement, which was then registered in the minutes of the synod meeting. The unification of the two bodies was complete.

Archbishop Michael had made his stand clear. "You be the metropolitan," he had told Philip. "I will relinquish my position." With his willingness not to be primate, Michael also stepped away from his seat on the Holy Synod and took his place as Archbishop Michael, auxiliary to Metropolitan Philip. His humility speaks highly of his character. He opted to serve, not to lead.

Not only was the reunification one of the very bright moments in the history of the Church of Antioch, it also brought congratulatory letters from Orthodox leaders of the other jurisdictions in North America. The members of the Standing Conference of Orthodox Bishops in America (SCOBA) offered an outpouring of gratitude to both archbishops, Philip and Michael, for the work they had done in the reunification process.

His dream to unite the two factions within Antioch complete, Philip told the delegates at the thirty-second convention of the archdiocese in 1975, "After sixty years of division and misunderstanding, our people are reunited. And there is no power on earth which will divide us again, because our unity is sealed in Christ."

The convention hall erupted into a prolonged standing ovation.

The fulfillment of this dream for unity

among the Arabic Orthodox Christians has given tangible hope for Philip's greater dream to be realized: the coming together of all of the Orthodox jurisdictions on the North American continent.

THE ORDER OF ST. IGNATIUS

Having traveled extensively in the archdiocese from 1966 to 1975, Philip noticed a dilemma. People with tremendous financial resources were not being challenged to give according to their means. Many gave little or nothing, and yet they had the potential to make the kinds of donations that could help influence the entire Church.

"I traveled from San Francisco to Los Angeles, from Montreal to Texas, from Florida to the Midwest. We have the most wonderful people in North America in our archdiocese," Philip reflected. "In talking with them I discovered that people will give if you identify the need and tell them clearly what you will do with the money you wish to raise. They will give."

In 1975 Philip conceived in his mind the Order of St. Ignatius of Antioch. St. Ignatius was the third bishop to preside over the Church in Antioch, serving from the years A.D. 67 to 107. He was an example of sacrifice, a martyr. He gave his life, the most precious thing he had, for the cause of Christ.

"Since we are historically from the Church of St. Ignatius," he told an initial gathering of potential members, "why don't we call this organization the Order of St. Ignatius?" Three levels of membership were discussed: $500 a year, $1,000 a year, or a $15,000 lifetime membership.

This time the dreamer faced a few doubting Thomases. One told him, "You'll be lucky if you find fifty people who will give you $500 a year." But Philip knew better because he knew his people. He was convinced if he told order members why he needed the money and how it would be used, they would participate.

"Wait and see," Philip told the doubter.

The first induction into the Order of St. Ignatius was in San Francisco during the archdiocesan convention of 1976, the tenth anniversary of Philip's consecration. Mr. Al Joseph, a business leader from Chicago, was selected as the first president. The Order of St. Ignatius started with thirty-six members. Would they grow beyond fifty? In 1991, the Order has significantly exceeded one thousand men and women.

The Order has funded two outreach programs designed to bring new people to Christ and His Church: the Department of Missions and Evangelism and the Department of Campus Ministry. At the encouragement of the metropolitan, the trustees of the archdiocese had established a clergy pension fund back in 1968, and from its inception the Order has contributed generously to that project. In under fifteen years, the Order of St. Ignatius has raised nearly $5 million for archdiocesan projects, for charities, and for projects at the patriarchate. It is an aggressive arm of the Church, a dynamic movement that continues to grow. Even the doubting Thomases have joined!

"He goes into everything like that," commented Father Joseph Allen, national chaplain of the Order. "He doesn't wait around long. The idea will come to him; he'll catch the vision, dream the dream—but then he'll go after it with full force."

And when does the metropolitan dream his dreams, cultivate his ideas? In the evenings. "I usually don't go any place at night," he says. "I stay at home.

"Many people think that since I live in such close proximity to Broadway, I should go out and see some of the long-running plays. When I travel, I see plenty of attractions, so when I come home I dream of new things. I am a dreamer and always have been. I thank God that most of the dreams have come true."

The Russian Connection

Then they said
among the nations,
"The LORD has done
great things for them."
The LORD has done
great things for us,
Whereof we are glad.

Psalm 126:2, 3

From his youth—and particularly during the years he served as secretary to Patriarch Alexander III—Philip had heard about the Church of Russia. Bishops in Damascus who had visited there returned home with almost incredible reports of how the Christian people were persevering with joy and dedication to their Lord in the face of cruel persecution.

He dreamed of one day seeing Russia for himself.

In early 1976 the late Patriarch of Moscow, Pimen, extended to Philip the metropolitan an invitation to tour the country and visit the churches and to bring with him a delegation of clergy from America. He immediately accepted the invitation and chose to accompany him Fathers Antoun Khouri, John Namie of Houston, and George S. Corey of Pittsburgh.

On Wednesday, September 29, 1976, the party met at the Aeroflot ticket counter at New York's Kennedy Airport in preparation for their departure to Moscow via London on the Soviet airline. Ted and Nellie Mackoul, Kathy Meyer, and Bill Essey of the archdiocesan office came out to the airport to say good-bye.

MOSCOW

The flight overseas was long and taxing. Because they were an official delegation, Philip and his party were able to move through customs without incident. Bishop Chrysostom, vice chairman of external affairs for the Russian Orthodox Church, met the tired American party as they deplaned, accompanied by one of Philip's life-long friends from Balamand days, Father Makarios Tayyar, who represented the Patriarchate of Antioch in Moscow. Natasha Gorina, who would serve as interpreter for Philip, was also on hand.

With the luggage stowed safely in the trunks of the cars, the motorcade headed toward downtown Moscow to the hotel for the start of the twelve-day tour. From the hotel window, Philip could look down onto a large public square. He counted six Orthodox Churches, all converted to museums by the Communist government.

"What a magnificent sight those Churches are," Philip said to Father Antoun. Both men wondered silently whether those beautiful structures would ever, in their lifetimes, be used again for Christian worship.

At dinner in the hotel dining room that Thursday evening, the tourists were surprised to find a small American flag at the head of the table. They felt conspicuous in the restaurant, with their black suits, clerical collars, and large pectoral crosses. The stares of the other guests made them know they were the center of attention.

On the next day, Friday, October 1, one of the first and very memorable incidents of the tour took place. After having stopped by the department of external affairs for a welcome and an exchange of gifts, the entourage was taken to visit several of the churches in Moscow, some in full use by Orthodox Christians and some converted to museums. Philip was impressed that even in the government-controlled museums, people could be seen standing before the icons in prayer to the Lord. The icons and the altar with the Gospel book on it were still in place in these "museums." These were often called "nonoperating churches," with a guardian present, who was employed by the state to watch over the facility.

"I remember approaching one of these nonoperating churches," Philip reminisces. "We were approved to tour it, so we bought our admission tickets and went inside. Everything was correctly in place, as though it were still an active church. I went straight into the sanctuary and kissed the Gospel book and the altar."

Suddenly, without warning, the woman

who was guarding this museum began to scream out at Philip in Russian, "What are you doing? What are you doing?"

"What is her problem?" Philip asked Father Makarios in Arabic.

"She thinks you are a layman going into the altar area through the royal doors," he said. "She has no idea you are an Orthodox archbishop."

Philip walked over to the woman and smiled at her. He showed her his pectoral icon, which a bishop always wears. It had been hidden beneath his topcoat. She knelt to the ground and said in Russian, "I am sorry," and she embraced the metropolitan.

Emotionally stirred by the exchange, Philip turned back toward the altar and in tears prayed for the people of Russia that one day they would know the freedom to worship God openly once again.

"That lady guard was an Orthodox Christian who wanted to protect the altar," Philip recalled. "That is why she reacted the way she did—and I loved it!"

The Americans noted that the Russian people did not smile much—until Friday afternoon when they were off work for the weekend. Then, the spirit of Moscow picked up noticeably. But for the Christian believers, those same smiles were visibly mingled with tears as they came to worship God on Sunday morning. "We witnessed people— thousands of them—crying during each Liturgy we attended," Philip recalled. "And virtually every ser-

Metropolitan Philip, center, with President Hafez Al-Assad of Syria at the right.

Below, with Pope John Paul II, and Cardinal Bernard Law of Boston.

Left: Metropolitan Philip breaking ground at Antiochian Village, 1983. Ernest Saykaly, vice-chairman of the board of trustees is at left. Clergy are Bishop Antoun and Father John Namie.

Below: Archbishop Michael Shaheen, left, with Metropolitan Philip.

With the Antiochian Women (AOCWNA), St. George Church, Toronto, 1982.

*With David Taweel, age
11 months, 1987.*

*Sharing a secret with Samia
Makhlouf, 1989.*

Above: the Consecreation of Bishop Antoun Khouri, 1985, with Father Basil Essey on the right.

Right: Saidna Philip with Father Joseph Allen, vicar-general of the Antiochian archdiocese.

Philip with President Amin Gamayel of Lebanon during their meeting in 1987.

With John Sununu, White House Chief of Staff, at the 1989 Antiochian convention in Los Angeles.

The Metropolitan's residence and Archdiocesan Headquarters in Englewood, NJ.

Clergy symposium, Antiochian Village, 1988.

Patriarch Ignatius IV speaks to a 1985 banquet during his visit to North America. At left are Ernest Saykaly and Metropolitan Philip.

The ordinations-chrismations of the AEOM clergy and faithful. Clergy are, from left, Metropolitan Philip, Fathers Jack Sparks, Peter Gillquist, Paul Romley.

His Eminence, Metropolitan Philip Saliba, Primate, Antiochian Orthodox Christian Archdiocese of North America.

mon preached by the Russian priests had to do with the Resurrection. The message was almost always, 'Do not ever give up hope.'"

LENINGRAD

On midnight Friday, the metropolitan and his party boarded the train for Leningrad. They arrived the next morning and were shown to a European-style downtown hotel where they were housed in the quaintest rooms of the trip. After breakfast Philip rested while the others toured the city.

Father George Corey and Father John Namie took to the streets to see something of this centuries-old city, formerly named St. Petersburg for Tsar Peter the Great. They had ridden the subway for several blocks, gotten off, and walked up the stairs to street level.

"We were standing there trying to decide what to do next," Father George recalls, "and there were three young men standing next to us on the corner. They turned to look at us and in broken English said, 'You must be Americans.' We said, 'Yes, we are.' And they said, 'Oh, wonderful.'

"I asked them how they knew we were Americans. They said, 'We can tell by the way you are dressed. You are pastors, aren't you?' They saw our clerical collars."

Father George explained to them that he and Father John were Orthodox Christian priests,

and that made them even happier. The three young
Russians invited the two priests to their home to
talk.

"But we don't know you, and you don't
know us," Father John Namie objected. "Let us invite you into this restaurant," he said, motioning to
a cafe two doors down, "and we'll sit and talk."

The five new acquaintances walked into the
establishment and talked for two or three hours. In
the course of the conversation, the young Russians
told the priests about themselves and how difficult
life was. They reminded the Americans, "Out of all
the millions of people in the Soviet Union, only a
small percentage are members of the Communist
Party. But they are in control of the government.

"One day the masses will overthrow the government," they predicted, "and the Church will
come out on top!" They even predicted that perhaps the Church would run the country for a few
years until there was a new government.

"We sat there in awe and drank in the conversation," Father George recalls. "We were saying,
'This is impossible! This will never happen!'

"They said, 'No, no, there was a revolution
in 1917. One of these days, brothers, you are going
to see another revolution here!'"

Two of the young men were Jewish; the
other was an Orthodox Christian. The Americans
sat in stunned silence.

About dinnertime Saturday, the entire visiting delegation was taken to the Holy Transfiguration Cathedral. There, Philip and the host bishop, Cyril, presided at an all-night vigil. Two thousand Christians stood for over three hours praying while the choir sang hymns in Slavonic, Arabic, and English. Philip preached on the oneness of Christians who share the true faith "in spite of the oceans which separate us, in spite of our different languages and culture, and in spite of our differing political systems."

With tears in their eyes, the people shouted out to him in Russian at the close of his message, "May God save you!"

The choir was magnificent. Most of the worshipers were elderly women, but there were a remarkable number of young people on hand as well. With the joy of this vigil service, the American party expectantly anticipated the glory of the Divine Liturgy the following morning.

On Sunday, October 3, Philip awoke to a bright sunlit morning. He dressed hurriedly in time to be picked up for his ride to St. Nicholas Cathedral where he was greeted by the ringing of the church's seventeen bells. Over one thousand people had gathered for worship in the lower level of the cathedral. Upstairs, some three thousand more were in attendance. The crowd moved sideways from the center of the nave to form a passageway for Metropolitan Philip, Bishop Cyril, and twelve priests and six deacons to enter.

In his written account of the trip, Father George Corey recorded, "What seemed only an hour Liturgy turned out to be three hours long. We knew we may never have such an experience again, so we filmed and taped as much as possible.

"The Liturgy was served in Slavonic, Arabic, and English, and the choir and deacons never missed one cue nor left out one iota! The service flowed magnificently to its glorious conclusions, recalling in my mind the words of the emissaries of Prince Vladimir in describing the Orthodox liturgy to him: We thought we had entered heaven itself."

In his sermon, Metropolitan Philip specifically thanked the Church in Russia for establishing Orthodox Christianity in America through the work of the eighteenth- and nineteenth-century Russian missionaries to Alaska, for sending those who came to California, and for giving America her first Orthodox saint, St. Herman of Alaska.

On the way to dinner on Sunday, Father Corey paused in the outside courtyard to distribute gifts of icons, Bibles, and crosses he had brought with him from his parish in Pittsburgh. Hundreds of the worshipers crowded around him, eager to receive his handouts and asking for his blessing. Father Antoun was scolding him from a distance, much to his dismay. Later in the car Father Antoun told Father George that what he was doing was patently illegal.

The following day, Monday, the Americans

were taken to some of Leningrad's famous museums, including the art museum, and then to several
historic Churches. At one of the great cathedrals,
which had once housed the miraculous Icon of our
Lady of Kazan, the Communist tour guide took
the opportunity to denounce the evils caused by
Christianity. It was Marxist propaganda in full
bloom. Her party line bashed Orthodox Christianity, Roman Catholicism, and protestantism, all
three. Then came the clincher, how communism
rescues the people from God Himself—all of this
spoken inside one of the greatest Christian sites in
Russia.

Father John Namie, inspired by the Holy
Spirit, thanked the guide for her tour. Then he said
to her compassionately, "May this same God
whom you condemn save you!"

On Wednesday, the distinction between the
Church and the world became apparent again as
the entourage visited the famous Riskariovakoye
Memorial Cemetery where the 650 thousand victims of the Nazi siege of Leningrad in 1941 and
1942 are buried. The guide who accompanied the
American group and who had been hired for her
job by the Communist party, stood nearby. When
they arrived at the foot of the huge statue *Mother
Russia,* Philip felt impressed to pray the Trisagion,
or thrice-holy prayers, requesting the mercy of the
Lord for those who were departed.

He called Fathers Antoun, John, and

George to his side, and began with the prayer, "Blessed is our God always, now and ever, and unto the ages of ages. Amen."

Immediately, the guide turned and hurriedly walked off. She stood away from the Christians at a noticeable distance. "I gathered from her actions and how swiftly she left us that she feared being photographed with us. Presumably, she was concerned with losing her job if she were seen praying," Philip said.

ZAGORSK

The next day, the delegation flew back to Moscow and bade farewell to their interpreter Natasha, who would be leaving them to escort Mrs. Nelson Rockefeller, wife of the vice president, who had arrived for her tour through Russia. Friday it was off to Zagorsk and the Trinity-Sergius Monastery which dates back to 1380. Philip was to celebrate the Divine Liturgy with Patriarch Pimen on the Feast Day of St. Sergius, and nearly thirty thousand people came out on this rainy, cold and gloomy day to pray!

Father George Corey wrote, "As we walked from place to place after the service, the faithful, standing in the rain, stopped the Metropolitan to receive his blessing. Many tears were shed as we witnessed the deeply pious devotion of the faithful. We left Zagorsk with a renewed commitment to our faith. We had seen devotion elsewhere, in

America and other parts of the world, but never like this. We learned a great deal about Christian faith in Holy Russia."

MOSCOW

At a special farewell luncheon, hosted by the department of external affairs of the patriarchate, Metropolitan Philip prayed prophetically that the great bells of the Kremlin Churches would one day ring again throughout the land, calling the faithful to worship. The bells had not rung since the Revolution of 1917.

He encouraged his fellow clergy and Orthodox laity to continue their witness to the person of Jesus Christ, "Who frees us from every political and social system." His Eminence reminded his hosts that because of this visit, "a new relationship now exists between Orthodox Christians of the Antiochian Church in North America and the great Russian Church."

Sunday, October 10, 1976, was departure day. Philip looked out of his hotel room window that morning for one last time. His eyes skipped across the Moscow skyline, dotted with its numerous Churches and golden cupolas. "There is no history of Russia without the history of the Orthodox Christian Church," he had reminded people at his every stop.

Snow flurries began to fall as the party left the hotel for the airport and the journey home.

"If I ever return to Russia," Philip told his
hosts at the air terminal, "I hope I will hear the
bells of the church at the Kremlin ringing, sum-
moning the people to come and worship Jesus
Christ. Someday the soft tears of your Christian
people will become mightier than the tyranny of
the state and wash away the indifference to God
among those who deny Him in this land!"

Someone tugged at Philip's coat. "Cut it
short!" he said. "You must not talk like that." It was
a priest whom Philip had suspected might be a
KGB front. He kept on staring angrily at the metropolitan, and he said forcefully, "These Churches
will *never* open to the people!"

IN RETROSPECT

"The tour of Russia was one of the most important trips I have ever made," Philip says, looking
back. "It was very emotional. I believe I cried every
day of the journey, at every service. There is something absolutely overwhelming hearing the thousands of people in the Church praying together. On
the wall of the apse, behind virtually every altar,
there is the icon of the Resurrection of Christ—it is
there in every Church. And every sermon I heard
preached centered on the Resurrection.

"I asked one of the priests, 'Why is there this
continual emphasis on the Resurrection?' He said
to me, 'We want to be prepared because someday,

in Christ, the Church will arise again! He will resurrect us to Himself.'

"I dare to believe this resurrection has begun under Mikhail Gorbachev."

Although the struggle for freedom in Russia is in its embryonic form and the situation could conceivably take a turn away from freedom, Philip is optimistic. "I am overjoyed by the turn of events at the opening of the 1990s in Eastern Europe, especially in Russia," he says. "The Russian Church could become free to resume its spiritual mission within the Orthodox world and internationally. The Russian Christians have so much to offer us through their rich tradition and their incomparable sacred music."

Unlike those of the secular historians and the global economists, Philip's assessments of Russia during and after his trip dealt with spiritual issues. "I felt that in Russia the struggle was not between communism and capitalism, though I believe in the free enterprise system. I always felt that communism was going to collapse anyway, even before we took this trip. The struggle in Russia is between Marx and Christ. And in the final analysis, Christ will be the victor."

While what has happened as the decade of the 90s opened in Russia and in Eastern Europe confirmed Philip's words to the people in 1976, in one sense the changes have taken him by surprise. "I didn't expect to see it so soon," he said. "I thought it was going to take perhaps another fifty years. But God has His own calendar. He works in mysterious ways. Now, here is Gorbachev, opening several thousand churches in the Soviet Union."

Then he added, "The bells have rung again, even in the Kremlin!"

12

Patriarchal Blessings

Blessed is he who comes in
the name of the LORD!

Psalm 118:26

It was called "an explosion of love." In 1977, for the first time in the history of the archdiocese, the Patriarch of Antioch was coming to visit his flock in North America.

Patriarch Elias IV had been elected head of the Church of Antioch in 1970, after the death of Theodosius VI. Philip had yearned to have him come, but he first wanted to see the two archdioceses of Toledo and New York brought together. Now, that had been accomplished.

Also, some difficulties between New York and Damascus had recently been solved. "It seems that somehow, beginning with the reign of every new Patriarch who has been elected since I've been metropolitan, I go through a difficult initial period with him. Patriarch Elias and I exchanged some pretty tough letters, and we had specific disagreements. But I had the utmost respect and love for him, and I wanted him to visit the archdiocese and bless our people." The official invitation to Patriarch Elias to visit the archdiocese was extended in late 1976.

Before he arrived, Philip raised half a million dollars to establish an endowment in the Patriarch's name to perpetuate theological education at the Balamand Seminary. Subsequently another hundred thousand dollars was added to it as a trust fund for the seminary. "If it weren't for that money," Philip recalls, "the school would have faced tremendous difficulties in view of the war that had been going on in Lebanon for the past several years."

Patriarch Elias arrived in New York on May 18, 1977. He was met at the plane by an enthusiastic crowd of Orthodox faithful. The sixty-three-year-old hierarch, white-haired and alive with zeal, spoke a brief word of greeting to those on hand to welcome him. Metropolitan Philip brought him back to archdiocesan headquarters and made sure he was comfortable. "We put him in the suite upstairs," Philip remembers, "and the plan was to let him rest a few days from his journey before beginning the tour."

Two days after the Patriarch's arrival, Philip was working downstairs in his office when suddenly he thought he heard a dog barking. He called Kathy. "Do we have a dog here in the house?"

"Yes, I hear it too, a barking noise," she said.

The barking was coming from up on the second floor. Going upstairs to investigate, they found Patriarch Elias engrossed in front of the television set, watching "Lassie" with the volume turned up. They discovered he watched "Lassie" whenever he had the chance.

ON TOUR

As the travel schedule began, including cities such as New York, Montreal, Boston and Worcester, Washington, Pittsburgh, Detroit, Louisville, Oklahoma City, and Los Angeles, thousands turned out to greet the Patriarch of Antioch. He had an immediate rapport with the Orthodox youth, recalling on one of his early stops, "When I was a very young man and just beginning my ministry in the Church, Patriarch Gregory Haddad handed me my first cassock saying, 'My son, this robe is given to you black. On the last day you will be asked to present it before the throne of God, whitened by a life of love, holiness, and good deeds.'"

One of the recurring themes of his preaching concerned the spiritual climate of service to Christ in the priesthood. Always the realist, the Patriarch was particularly frank about his feelings in one memorable interview.

"A priest must always be a preacher of the truth, without fear of any power or person, be he rich or poor, powerful or weak. He must not only preach the good news of Jesus Christ to the people; he must first and foremost be an icon of this message before them."

Never one to deny the presence of problems,

he went on to talk with the reporter about pastoral priorities: "Today's priest, like all humanity, is surrounded by a deluge of temptation. He must reaffirm every second of his life that Jesus Christ is his first and only consideration. The priesthood is not a job, but a totally sacrificial way of life."

He concluded his remarks with the fire of a man on a mission: "An unbelieving or uncertain priesthood is of the greatest danger to the body of Christ. Everyone, including priests, has the right to the good and blessed things of God's creation. However, a priest must never permit himself to set these good things as his final goal, and he must remind those in his charge of the same. He must not let himself be a slave to anything except to the person of our crucified Lord."

"We traveled together to each of the regional parish life conferences," Philip remembers. "It was a very exciting experience for everyone to hear him and meet him. Although he didn't speak English very well, he had this special charisma—and such a bright face and active gestures. He was a very spontaneous man."

LOS ANGELES

When the hierarchs reached Los Angeles, the parish life conference was led by Father Paul Romley, pastor at St. Nicholas Cathedral. "What can we give the Patriarch, what can we do for him while he's here, to make his visit especially memorable?" Father Paul asked the metropolitan.

"I have an idea," Philip answered. "Invite Lassie to the closing banquet."

"What on earth are you talking about?" asked Father Paul.

Philip told his priest about the barking dog incident. Father Paul made appropriate calls to friends in the film industry, and Lassie was scheduled to come to the grand banquet of the conference.

The Patriarch, of course, knew nothing about the plan. Lassie, being a Hollywood star, was housed in a kennel nearby. The night of the banquet was at hand.

Philip, who was master of ceremonies, stopped the banquet proceedings at the appropriate point. Escorted by her handler, in walked Lassie, down the center aisle and all the way up to the podium where the patriarch was seated. He was absolutely speechless, his dark brown eyes following her every move in unbelief. She turned around to face the roaring crowd and gave Patriarch Elias an envelope she held in her mouth. Then she jumped up and put her front paws on his shoulders and kissed him.

Lassie turned back to deafening applause and came down to the front of the podium. She looked back at the Patriarch, greeted him with a short farewell bark, and went out the rear door of the banquet hall.

Patriarch Elias was ecstatic. "I have never seen him so excited," Philip smiled. "He just kept saying, 'Lassie, Lassie!' He was utterly overwhelmed, and the people absolutely loved it."

The conference was a rare blessing for all. Patriarch Elias powerfully exemplified his patron saint, Elias in the Old Testament. Both were zealous men, and he had the zeal and the spontaneity of his namesake.

"I will return to the see bearing your love. And I will pray to our Lord Jesus Christ every morning and every evening that He may lengthen your days, preserve your children, and fill your hearts always with the spirit of love and unity, as you are shepherded by Metropolitan Philip, blessed of God, who has dedicated his very life to Christ and His holy Church," he told the people. "God bless each of you."

BACK EAST

From Los Angeles the Patriarch and his party flew on to Pittsburgh where he was to preside over the Eastern Region parish life conference. He was so tired by the time he reached his destination he could barely deplane. Inside the Pittsburgh terminal a huge crowd was on hand for a surprise reception, and the press showed up *en masse*. TV cameras were rolling and the journalists had their pads and pencils ready.

One of the reporters said to him, "Your Beatitude, we hear that next week you are going to visit President Carter at the White House. What are you going to talk with him about?"

With fatigue written across his face and with no strength or desire for late-night interviews, he answered, "Nothing."

Metropolitan Philip was beside himself. "Your Beatitude," he said in Arabic, "You cannot say 'Nothing' to the American press! Tomorrow there will be headlines in the Pittsburgh papers that Elias IV will say 'Nothing' to President Carter! Here in the United States, they print *everything* you say. If you breathe, they will show it on television."

Elias IV changed his mind and granted a brief interview. "Yes, I am going to discuss the Middle East situation with him, to see if we can bring peace to that war-torn area." With his answer he explained to the reporters that he was tired, and he asked for their understanding.

During his trip to Washington, the Patriarch indeed visited with the president, discussing with him both the Orthodox Christian faith, and the plight of the Palestinian refugees in the Middle East. Then, on July 26, he opened that day's session of the U.S. Senate with this prayer:

O Lord Jesus Christ our God, the God of mercies and blessings, whose mercy is limitless and whose love for mankind surpasses understanding: bowing our heads in adoration before Your majesty, with fear and trembling as unworthy servants and humbly rendering thanks unto Your lovingkindness for Your blessings bestowed upon Your people, we glorify You, we praise You, we sing to You, and we magnify You as our only Lord and Master.

And since You have graciously accepted the prayers of Your servants and have fulfilled them, so also grant that from this time this land and all lands may be delivered from want and may be blessed with peace, tranquility, and brotherhood, that increasing in true love of You, Your people may receive all Your benefits.

Furthermore we pray for the president of the United States, his vice president and cabinet, the members of this senate and for all civil authorities. Grant that they may work diligently to achieve Your peace, insuring liberty, justice, and freedom for all mankind. For this and all Your blessings, we offer thanksgiving unto You, together with Your Father who is from everlasting, and Your all-holy, good, and life-giving Spirit; saying, Glory to You, O God our Benefactor, unto ages of ages. Amen.

A major theme both of his speeches and interviews was the connection between salvation and social outreach in the New Testament. "The Church must educate her people to the gospel precepts of justice, freedom, mercy, love, and charity. In this way the Church can and must influence the political process, but only by influencing individuals and bringing them to a knowledge of Jesus Christ," he told his listeners.

In Montreal, another media incident happened. The Divine Liturgy was to be televised all over the area. Philip reminded the Patriarch before the service began, "You have to watch all your movements, because we are going to be live on TV."

All went well at the outset. When the Patriarch received the chalice after the Great Entrance, he began to pray for those who had departed. Metropolitan Kurban wanted him to remember an additional name that had not been written on the piece of paper in front of him. His cadence was interrupted. With the TV camera focused on him for all Canada to see, the Patriarch turned to the metropolitan and said, "Get off my back!" Fortunately, he spoke in Arabic.

In Oklahoma City, the Patriarch was speaking to a banquet of over eight hundred people. Metropolitan Philip was serving as his translator. As he was addressing the people, he used an expression from an Arabic proverb which says, "I love my beloved, even though he is a black slave." It echoed the poetic flow of the Song of Solomon in the Old Testament.

Philip looked up and in a split second realized that many of the waiters at the dinner were black, and he knew it would be confusing and insulting to them were he to translate the proverb. "It immediately became a humorous thing for me because I knew, either way, I would lose. Every time I translated for him, we had an argument as it was. So I simply stopped the translation."

Elias looked at Philip and said sternly, "Translate."

"I can't translate that, Your Beatitude." Philip quickly explained to him the implication of the statement, and the Patriarch agreed to go on with his speech.

THE CALL FOR UNITY

At the national convention in 1977, Patriarch Elias spoke of his efforts in the U.S. and Canada and throughout the Orthodox world to bring about jurisdictional unity in North America. He called the move "inevitable."

Metropolitan Philip had underscored the importance of such a move during a message on Orthodoxy Sunday at the beginning of Lent in 1977 at the Greek Orthodox Cathedral of the Holy Trinity. In a story released by Religious News Service (RNS) his proposal was "to transform the Standing Conference of Canonical Orthodox Bishops in the Americas into a governing body for an autonomous Orthodox Church." The news account went on to say,

Speaking of the several overlapping North American Orthodox jurisdictions—"which

fundamentally contradicts our canonical and
ecclesiological teachings"—Metropolitan
Philip said the Synod he proposes "will be able
to speak to America and the world with one
voice and one accord."

Then came the part of the proposal which
attracted the most attention.

The Antiochian leader added that the
Synod's most important task would be "preparation for the establishment of a future Orthodox Patriarchate in America which will reflect
both our organic unity and the richness and
diversity of our ethnic cultures. I want to make
it clear that this patriarchate can only be established by a common decision of all Orthodox churches."

He concluded his remarks with this assessment:

Orthodoxy, despite her past glory, remains the best kept secret in this land because
of our failure to understand the missionary di-
mensions of the Church.

America does not understand us because
we are still talking to her in languages which
she does not understand. We are still talking to
America as Greeks, Russians, Serbians, Ukra-

nians, Romanians, etc. No wonder then that six million Orthodox have no presence on the American scene."

A lead story in *The National Herald* carried a negative response: "Strong protests, both here and in Greece, followed the statement made by Metropolitan Philip Saliba of Antioch regarding the creation of a Synod for Eastern Orthodoxy in North America, 'with the blessing of the Mother Churches.'"

But both Patriarch Elias and Metropolitan Philip remained undeterred, calling for Orthodox unity wherever they went. To this day, Philip believes that one Orthodox jurisdiction in America must happen. "To settle for less is heresy," he believes.

DEPARTURE

The patriarchal visit had a significant spiritual impact on the Antiochian Orthodox people. It was the first time they had seen the Patriarch of Antioch on North American soil. "Our lives will never be the same," Philip said. "He is absolutely real."

Patriarch Elias stayed with his people from May to August. As the patriarchal visit concluded, Philip wrote, "For two and one half months the presence of His Beatitude transfigured this Archdiocese from 'glory to glory.' He traveled to Canada and throughout the United States and presided over our convocations. Thousands of our people had the opportunity to kiss his hand, to receive his blessing, an experience which they will never forget."

Not two years later newspaper headlines across North America carried sad news. "Millions Mourn Death of Orthodox Christian Leader," announced the *Montreal Gazette*.

"The day Elias IV died was one of the saddest days of my life," Philip said. "June 21, early in the morning, I went to the dining room to eat breakfast. The deacon was awaiting me. I told him I had spent a restless night, and I even heard the phone ring about four. He looked at me with tears in his eyes, but did not say a word.

"When I finished breakfast, the deacon said with a shaky voice, 'The phone call which you heard this morning was from Damascus. The Patriarch is dead.' We looked at each other and with much grief burst into tears."

Patriarch Elias IV had succumbed to a massive heart attack at his home in Damascus on June 21, 1979. Philip and a delegation of priests including Father Antony Gabriel of Montreal left immediately for Syria.

"He was a modern John Chrysostom in his fiery sermons," said Father Antony in the June 30 issue of the *Gazette*. "He preached up and down the Middle East, and wherever he went he drew thousands of people.

"He was a champion of the poor and the oppressed, and he lived very simply himself. When you met him, you felt like you had encountered a saint."

Philip and his entourage remained in Damascus to participate in the election of the new Patriarch. The leading candidate was Metropolitan Ignatius Hazim who had served for years as the dean of the theological school at Balamand. On July 2, 1979, the fifty-nine-year-old educator was chosen 166th successor to the throne of Saints Peter and Paul in Antioch. On July 8 he was installed amidst joyous celebration in the Cathedral in Damascus.

13

The Dreamer,
the Doer

But without your consent I wanted to do nothing, that your good deed might not be by compulsion, as it were, but voluntary.

Philemon 14

Shortly after Patriarch Elias IV had left the country to return to Damascus, Father Antoun asked to see Philip. After eight years assisting the metropolitan at headquarters, from 1969 to 1977, Antoun wanted to return full time to the priesthood and to parish life.

"St. Nicholas Cathedral in Brooklyn is a possibility," Philip told him, "but I need you here until you find me someone to take your place."

ARCHDEACON HANS

Hans El-Hayek came from Lebanon in the mid 1970s to study at St. Vladimir's and was ready to graduate. He had worked two summers at the Englewood headquarters to earn money for school and had done everything from filing letters to gardening. Everyone had been impressed with his performance. "I believe Hans could do the job, Saidna," Antoun said. "Keep an eye on him for the next couple of weeks and see what you think."

Near the end of August, Philip called out to Hans, who was working in the yard, and asked him to come in. They went upstairs to talk in the study.

"You might have heard that Father Antoun is going to leave here to take a parish," Philip began. "I would like you to begin working for me in his place."

Hans was pleasantly shocked—and fearful. He had held the metropolitan in high esteem during the past two summers. Particularly he had been encouraged by the personal interest Philip had taken in him, with the metropolitan asking on several occasions if he had adequate money for tuition, books, and clothes.

"Saidna, I don't know whether I will be able to do this job," Hans answered, "but I will try my best to do it."

"I don't want you to say only that you will try," responded the metropolitan. "I want you to say that you are going to try *and* that you are going to succeed!"

Hans remembers, "Those were his exact words, and they still ring in my ears." He began work on September 1, 1977, and has served in exemplary fashion as personal deacon to the metropolitan ever since. He was elevated to archdeacon in 1987.

Says Philip concerning him, "He is the most humble and gracious man I have ever known."

PHILIP THE EVANGELIST

In 1978 Philip chose as his text for his annual message to the general assembly in Houston, Texas, "These who have turned the world upside down have come here too," from Acts 17:6. He proclaimed 1978 as "The Year of Mission" in the Antiochian Orthodox archdiocese.

Philip exhorted his flock to upgrade their own level of commitment to the Lord before attempting to reach out to others. "Self-evangelization means bringing the gospel of Jesus Christ to yourself first. If we are not converted on a personal basis, how can we convert others to Christ? Christ's commandment to 'Go and make disciples of all nations,' is true today as it was yesterday and it shall be until the end of history. Those of us who neglect this commandment betray the essence of the Christian message."

Then he aimed his remarks toward revitalization of the parishes. "It is not enough to build beautiful and adequate facilities for the Church to meet and glorify God. To revitalize our communities means to bring each and every one in the parish to the fellowship of Christ."

In his messages, the metropolitan thrives on getting down to cases. "I asked one of my priests once: 'Father, why don't you go after these seventy-five families who have dropped out of your parish and bring them back to Christ?' He said: 'Saidna, they are no good.' I said: 'This is precisely why you should minister to them. If they are no good, it is our duty to make them good.' Our Lord said: 'Those who are well have no need of a physician, but those who are sick; I came not to call the righteous but sinners.'"

"I love his messages," says Ted Mackoul, the trustee of the archdiocese who oversees finances. "He never goes above your head. When he finishes, he always gets a thunderous standing ovation."

And he did on this occasion. But his messages go beyond words, toward progress, toward results. Ted Mackoul recalls, "In 1966, when he was consecrated, there were 60 parishes in the archdiocese and 86 clergy. By his 15th anniversary in the episcopate, there were 130 parishes and 200 clergy." The annual budget during that same fifteen-year period burgeoned from $77,000 to $1,066,000.

In talking mission, Philip Saliba is careful never to separate salvation of the body from that of the soul. His goal is to minister to the whole person. "I am very devoted to him for one very good reason," says Father George S. Corey, dean of the St. Nicholas Cathedral in Brooklyn. "I love the man because he has heart. People who know him sense the deep feeling coming from the heart of the man, reaching out to others. He is very compassionate.

"Since Metropolitan Philip's episcopacy within his archdiocese," Father Corey continues, "we have moved into areas of community life and

Church life and have brought new hope to the world that we had not been able to do before. I believe it is because of Saidna Philip's concern for the downtrodden, the homeless, the refugees, the displaced people who are in dire need.

"I know he helps students and other people who come to his door for assistance or through letters he receives. He does it quietly. These are things we do not publish on the pages of *The Word* or in *Again* magazine, things that are never mentioned. He takes gifts that people give him, and, instead of putting the money in the bank, he gives it to those in need. I think he will go down in history as a man who, beyond his great leadership ability, simply has heart."

ANTIOCHIAN VILLAGE

Since 1975, Philip dreamed of a place, far from the cities, where the Orthodox young people could go for a time of fellowship together, perhaps a camp or retreat center. During the 1970s Philip had watched carefully the social upheaval and student unrest in America. And besides the growing drug problem, the breakdown in home and family life had accelerated. He envisioned a place where the youth and their families could worship together and where respect for parents, the schools, and the Church could be instilled.

In late 1977, Father George M. Corry, pastor of St. Michael Church in Greensburg, Pennsylvania, called to say a Presbyterian camp was about to come on the market near Ligonier, in the mountainous region of Western Pennsylvania. Its three hundred acres of land included a lake, a large chapel, an olympic-sized pool, a field for baseball and volleyball, and cabins enough to house fifty campers.

Philip drove to the camp to look it over. He was immediately drawn to it. "It needs some renovation, but I love the place," he told Father George. "And these hills are beautiful. Why don't you sit down and negotiate with the sellers."

The owners had asked $400 thousand and Father George was able to arrive at a price of $350 thousand. With some opposition, the trustees decided to make a firm offer at that price, and it was accepted. The purchase was transacted in 1978, which meant that the first camping season at Antiochian Village would be early summer, 1979.

"My immediate choice for camp director is Father John Namie," Philip told his trustees. "He has a great way with kids."

"But I don't know anything about camping," Father John protested to Philip the next week.

"You are an industrious person who can learn about camping," Philip assured him. "All you really have to do is take good care of the kids when they come."

And come they did. The first year brought with it a full camping program, including daily matins and vespers—and quality food. The program was an instant success. Father John had done the job, and everyone was pleased.

"The kind of love these kids experience at the village, some of them never had even in their own homes," Philip observes. "The saddest day on the mountain is when the children pack up and we break camp. They are hugging and kissing Father John and each other, and everyone is crying."

The spirit of "Summer at the Village" caught on immediately with the youth—so much so that ten years after camp opened, when the first campers were college students, they pointed to summers at camp as the high point in their spiritual lives. In a planning meeting for campus ministry with Father Jon Braun, students were asked what they would like to experience as Christians on campus.

"What we would like would be Antiochian Village 365 days a year," one former camper replied.

"Every time I go to the mountain, I experience something new in my spiritual life," the metropolitan notes. "Often at the village, we will celebrate the Divine Liturgy outdoors with the mountains and the trees behind us, and the kids praying and singing the hymns together. You can almost reach out and touch the glory of the Lord."

Although the people of the archdiocese are solidly behind the project now, it was not always so. "Some dreams are tough to fulfill," Philip says philosophically. "All these facilities were ours for

$350 thousand, but still some of the board voted against the purchase. In a democracy everyone is entitled to an opinion. And that's fine. But over the years, I've noticed God always wins these elections!"

With the camping program off and running, Philip's next dream was something for the parents. Under the leadership of Ernest Saykaly of Montreal, vice president of the board of trustees, this dream was fulfilled with a fifty-room lodging facility (just expanded in 1990 to total one hundred rooms), a chapel, and later a Heritage and Learning Center housing valued books, icons, and Orthodox cultural artifacts in a beautiful library/museum setting. The center with its hotel and dining facilities is used by Orthodox Christians of all jurisdictions throughout the East, and it is becoming known as a conference center for local business and industry meetings in the off season.

"Ernest Saykaly has done a remarkable job in spearheading the village and in giving leadership to the entire board of trustees," Philip observes. "He is Mr. Efficiency." The Canadian business leader was elected to the board in 1974 and elected by the board of trustees as vice chairman in 1979 upon the retirement of the previous vice chairman, Monsour Laham of Boston.

What motivates people like Ernest Saykaly and his wife Vivian, already overbooked in their business and parish life in Montreal, to work, give, and travel on behalf of the archdiocese as well?

"It is Philip Saliba, the man," answers Saykaly without hesitation. "He motivates me like no one else I have ever known. In addition to being our metropolitan and a Christian leader, he is an absolutely astute businessman. He is sensitive, compassionate. He knows exactly what he wants and how to get that accomplished. I have tremendous confidence in his leadership."

A NEW BISHOP

With the expansion of Antiochian Village, the growing number of new missions, and the increased number of clergy who had been ordained to serve them, Philip put the need for another bishop to help him before his people at the 1981 convention. On August 1, 1981, they nominated three qualified clergy for the office of auxiliary bishop for the archdiocese. Antoun Khouri received the largest number of votes. This nomination was made according to the tradition of the Church and carefully followed the constitution and the tradition of the patriarchate of Antioch.

Ever since his visit to North America, Patriarch Elias had become increasingly committed to the spread of Orthodox Christianity in the West. And he knew that would take more strenuous oversight on Philip's part. But with the Patriarch's death in 1979 and with a certain provincialism remaining among some members of the patriarchal synod in Damascus, progress toward growth seemed to revert back to a crawl.

Philip and the patriarchate exchanged a vol-

ley of heated letters. Antioch was reluctant to consecrate a new bishop. Things reached a stalemate,
and at one point there were even rumblings of se-
cession by the American Church. The main issue:
do the clergy and laity have the right to nominate
their bishops? The people had put forth three episcopal candidates, and they could not even get a re-
jection of the slate from Damascus. After nearly a
year had elapsed, there was still no answer at all. It
was the August Storm of 1966 revisited.

Two of the patriarchal synod members had
lived in North America when they were priests.
Philip had a meeting with them. He made his point
with an All-American example of personal frustration.

"Say you drive up to a traffic light at a major
intersection," Philip imagined with them. "The
light is red. What do you do?"

"You stop," said one of the metropolitans.

"That's right—but how long do you stop?"
Philip countered.

"Well, until the light turns green," they said.

"Okay, and what if the light doesn't turn
green?" Philip kept probing.

"What do you mean?"

"I mean, what if you just sit there and the
light stays red?" Philip asked. "Suppose the light
won't turn green. What do you do? Will you wait
forever at the red light?"

"Well, no, you don't," one man answered.
"You look right and left, and if nobody is coming,
you go through the intersection."

"Precisely," said Philip. "I have made my point. I'll wait until the synod meets in early November. If the light has not turned green by then, I'm driving through the red light."

The dreamer was wide awake, and the patriarchal synod knew it. They met on November 4, 1982, in Damascus and elected Antoun Khouri the new auxiliary bishop.

In December Patriarch Ignatius IV issued the following statement:

> We felt that circumstances at one time or another have dictated to us that our people no longer participate with us, the clergy, in finding the effective, reasonable, spiritual leadership; namely, the nomination and election of bishops. We have decided henceforth that the spiritual leadership in the Patriarchate of Antioch will be a leadership chosen by and acceptable to the people. . . . Our theological point of view is: The Church is all of its people and not merely one group alone.

The red light officially turned green.

On January 9, 1983, Archimandrite Antoun Khouri was elevated to the rank of the holy episcopate to serve as auxiliary to Metropolitan Philip. His elevation was a moment of transfiguration for the entire archdiocese. More than fifteen hundred people filled St. Nicholas Cathedral of Brooklyn and its hall. All the national organizations of the archdiocese were well represented.

Philip was exuberant as he addressed the 1983 convention in Toronto: "Sunday, January 9, was an unforgettable day in the history of our archdiocese, and perhaps it was our finest hour. All of us who were there felt a tremendous outpouring of the Holy Spirit. Our hearts and minds were captured by a sense of the supernatural. Once again, Bishop Antoun, we say to you in ancient Greek from the depths of our hearts, *Axios! Axios! Axios!* You are worthy!"

MEETING THE PRESIDENTS

Over the years of his episcopate, Philip has paid pastoral calls on five presidents. In most conversations, the primary subject was the crisis in the Middle East. With Lyndon Johnson, in 1968, he felt he accomplished the least.

He also met Dwight Eisenhower in Palm Springs in 1968, eight years after the president's retirement from office. Eisenhower believed economic stability would solve the problems. He had sent envoys to the Middle East to encourage economic development in the area. "But the Palestinians don't want money," Philip told the former president. "They want to go home." The people loved their land and wanted it back.

"Somehow I felt he missed that point," Philip recalled later. "He reasoned like a general still, and pragmatic solutions alone have never solved the problem."

Meeting Gerald Ford, Philip brought several

Middle East leaders with him to the White House. They visited in the spring of 1976, during the war in Lebanon between the Palestinian leftists and the Maronites. "Please use your good office to halt this war," Philip urged him. "Is there some way you can intervene to stop the bloodshed?"

"If you're asking me to send troops to Lebanon," Ford answered, "I will never do that." The U.S. had just pulled out of Vietnam, and the administration needed no new military action. "But what if we permit a limited Syrian intervention?" the president suggested.

A specific step had to be taken to deter the spread of the Lebanese conflict, and the leaders agreed this solution might be best. Three days later, the White House issued a statement that the U.S. would not object to a temporary Syrian military presence in Lebanon to stop the loss of life. A successful intervention followed shortly thereafter.

During the visit of Patriarch Elias to North America, he and Philip called on President Jimmy Carter. There seemed to be an instant rapport, and Carter was eager to find a lasting solution to the Middle East conflict.

"He was extremely gracious and friendly to us, and I was impressed with his knowledge of the Holy Scriptures," Philip recalls. "He and the Patriarch discussed the biblical account of Abraham and Sarah honoring the people who were native to what we call the Holy Land, and Carter agreed with Patriarch Elias in his assessment.

"But frankly, I feel Carter found the wrong

solution to the Middle East crisis by isolating Egypt from the rest of the Arab world and asking only that nation to sign the Camp David Accord. The step, though admirable, has never worked."

With Ronald Reagan, Philip found himself discussing the book of Revelation and the second coming of Christ. "He was taken with prophecy, almost to the point of date setting, but was not much taken with the Middle East problem as such," Philip observed.

"I'm going to see King Hussein of Jordan shortly," the metropolitan explained to the president. "He is in close touch with the Palestinians, and the two groups are talking about jointly approaching Israel to seek peace."

"Tell President Assad to withdraw his Syrian troops from Lebanon," the president advised, "and give President Gemayel of Lebanon my best."

ANOTHER JOURNEY EAST

On April 8, 1983, Philip left for the Middle East accompanied by Fathers John Badeen and George Rados. It was another try for peace. When they reached Amman, Jordan, they were informed by the Jordanian ministry of information that the talks between King Hussein and Yasir Arafat had broken down, a setback to President Reagan's initiative of September 1, 1982.

The following Tuesday, on very short notice, Philip met with President Assad for two hours. They discussed issues related to Lebanon and the Middle East. President Assad unequivocally stated that if and when the Israelis withdrew from Lebanon without infringing on Lebanese sovereignty, he would immediately withdraw his army from Lebanon. "I was very much impressed by his sincerity and friendliness," Philip remarked.

On Wednesday the delegation flew to Lebanon and was received by Metropolitan Elias Audi of Beirut, other metropolitans of Lebanon, and many government officials. The news media covered their movements throughout Lebanon on a daily basis. On Friday, April 15, they met with the president of Lebanon, Amin Gemayel. Friday afternoon, a meeting was held with all the Orthodox archbishops of Lebanon and their lay representatives at the archbishopric of Beirut to distribute funds raised by the archdiocese of North America to the refugees of Lebanon. Money was given to non-Orthodox people as well as to Orthodox Christians.

Philip gave the 1983 convention his impressions. "The psychological and sectarian wounds are very deep, and they need a long time to heal. Almost all Lebanese villages, let alone the cities, have been affected by the war. The devastation which we saw reminds us of Stalingrad and Berlin at the end of the Second World War.

"The majority of the Lebanese people, however, still want a free and a united Lebanon. In the final analysis, the future of Lebanon depends on the outcome of the regional struggle between Israel and the Arab countries and the international struggle between the Soviet Union and the free world."

Unfortunately, his assessment has thus far proven correct. The changes in the Soviet Union offer guarded hope for the Middle East, but with the Arab-Israeli conflict in full bloom and with the added tension of the Iraqi invasion of Kuwait, the chances for lasting peace at the outset of the 1990s still seem remote.

A FAREWELL TO FATHER ALEXANDER

A giant in American Orthodoxy in the latter half of the twentieth century was Father Alexander Schmemann, dean of St. Vladimir's Seminary. For years, he and Philip had maintained their close and growing friendship.

In the early 1980s, Father Schmemann was diagnosed as having cancer. Among the last of his public appearances was at the 1983 Antiochian convention in Toronto, in which he received the Antonian Gold Medal of Merit from Metropolitan Philip. In his address, Father Alexander said:

When invited to speak here tonight, I received no instructions of any kind. I was free to choose my theme. But as I began to think about it, trying to go beyond the usual superfi-

cial banquet optimism, someone told me that
the guiding biblical text of this convention was
to be 1 Peter 2:9: "You are a chosen generation, a royal priesthood, a holy nation, His
own special people." Immediately my search
came to an end, in the first place because this
is one of my favorite texts, and in the second
place, because I cannot think of any biblical
text more appropriate to our many ecclesiastical problems.

I do not know whether all my contempo-
raries in the Church would agree with me in
saying that, at the end of the fifties and in the
sixties, all of the Orthodox churches in America were going through a kind of renaissance. I
say "a kind of" because I am not sure that "renaissance" is the appropriate word here.

But whether it is appropriate or not, I am
sure that something significant was happening
in the Church—a new hope, a new vision, a
new experience of the Church.

His call that night was as clear as it was pre-
dictable. As always, especially in his later years, he
was after one Orthodox jurisdiction in North
America:

Dear fellow Orthodox, I wish to share
with you my certitude [that we have] the beginning of a new era in the life of the Church,
a new ascension into the mystery of unity.

Five months later, December 13, 1983, Father Alexander died peacefully at home, his wife, Julianna, at his side. He was just sixty-two. His friend and confidant, Philip Saliba, gave the homily at the service of burial December 15. It reflected on Father Alexander's enormous contribution to Orthodoxy in America.

Father Schmemann was a pioneer in the field of liturgical theology, and I would dare say he is the father of liturgical theology in the Orthodox Church. His relentless emphasis on the eucharistic experience as a journey to the kingdom created a spiritual renaissance in thousands of parishes throughout the Orthodox world.

I was fortunate to have been one of his students. He has touched my life as well as many lives in this country and abroad. No matter how serious the subject was, Father Schmemann would always inject his wit and humor and make it most interesting. He made God, the Church, the sacraments, the liturgy, and even Byzantine history very much alive in our minds.

His burning desire was to see Orthodoxy organically united in North America. Unfortunately, he died before the realization of his dream. We shall continue to struggle for this unity, and we shall dedicate our efforts to the blessed memory of Father Alexander Schmemann.

Philip concluded his remarks saying,

Farewell, my dear friend. I am sure you have already heard these divine words: "Well done, thou good and faithful servant. You have been faithful over a little. I will set you over much. Enter into the joy of your Master."

HERITAGE AND LEARNING CENTER

Never content to stand on past victories, Philip had plans not only to use Antiochian Village as a camp for children and a retreat center for adults, he envisioned a Heritage and Learning Center there as well.

In that light, he chose the words of St. Paul to challenge his flock to support the project: "He who sows sparingly will also reap sparingly, and he who sows bountifully will also reap bountifully. So let one give as he purposes in his heart, not grudging or of necessity; for God loves a cheerful giver. And God is able to make all grace abound toward you, that you, always having all sufficiency in all things, have an abundance for every good work" (2 Cor. 9:6–8).

Philip still believed, as he had a decade earlier when he founded the Order of St. Ignatius, if you tell people why it is you want them to give and explain how you will use their gifts, they will respond with generous help. On July 15, in the presence of more than one thousand faithful, Philip broke ground for the center.

The Heritage and Learning Center is a living memorial to your parents and grandparents who planted the seeds of Orthodoxy in this North American soil and fought valiantly to preserve our eternal ideals and principles. And if some of you still ask, "Why the Center?" the answer is this: We must realize once and for all that we are on the threshold of the twenty-first century. The third millennium will be upon us more swiftly than the twinkling of an eye.

The center houses one of the finest Orthodox libraries in the world and a beautiful collection of icons, and it sponsors a school of iconography.

BLESSINGS

"By the time Saidna Philip worked through the election of Bishop Antoun with the synod in Damascus, things took a visible turn for the better," said Ted Mackoul, the energetic financial officer of the archdiocese. "The synod grew to respect him. From that time on, Saidna developed an excellent relationship with the Patriarch and the members of the holy synod."

In sports, it's called momentum, on Wall Street it's a bull market, and in education it is excellence. In the Church, it's called renewal. That is, there are both apostolic succession and apostolic success. The blessing of God upon Philip Saliba was becoming evident to all.

The archdiocese was on strong financial footing, with a beautiful headquarters chancery and a stunning conference center. The reorganization had taken hold with effective and productive departmental management. New missions sprang up throughout the seventies and early eighties, and the clergy were secure and at peace. Internally, the archdiocese was living out the dreams of its primate and running well—extremely well.

Other Orthodox leaders had taken notice. Philip was asked to serve alongside Archbishop Iakovos of the Greek archdiocese, the president of the Standing Conference of Orthodox Bishops in America (SCOBA) as the vice president of that body. Metropolitan Theodosius, primate of the Orthodox Church in America (OCA), invited Philip to serve as vice president of St. Vladimir's Seminary and in 1981 conferred on him an honorary doctorate of divinity.

Philip's vision was clear. Two things remained undone. These tasks were no secret to anyone—his fellow bishops knew them, as did his priests, his laity, and his trustees. Ted Mackoul enumerated the first challenge.

"All of us in this archdiocese long to see the administrative unity of the various Orthodox jurisdictions in North America. Orthodox Christianity will never fully impact this continent if there is not unity. We say we have it, but we don't," Mackoul admits frankly.

But is there hope? If the Orthodox of Antioch—New York and Toledo—were able to unite, can't that happen with the Greeks, the OCA, the Antiochians, the Serbians, the Romanians, and the other great national groupings of Orthodox Christians in North America?

"Absolutely!" says Mackoul. "This is our firm hope."

Father Gabriel Ashie is pastor of a large pan-Orthodox congregation, St. Luke's of Garden Grove, California. He knows where unity must come. "The fact is, we've got such incredible unity already in America. All Orthodox Christians believe exactly the same thing doctrinally and have since the days of the New Testament. We worship God the same way. The Divine Liturgy which we share in common has not altered in hundreds of years. Those areas are absolutely set. What we lack is administrative unity."

"And it is heresy, really, to be under separate primates in North America," enjoins Philip. "Two archbishops over a country, more than one bishop in a city, has been soundly condemned as error by a

Church council. The heresy is called *philetism,* separating from each other by national groupings. It is unique to our situation. There is no such thing as three canonical Orthodox jurisdictions in Lebanon, four in Greece, five in Russia. In God's time, there will be one in North America. Unity is inevitable.

"We have a marvelous opportunity in America to dream dreams and see visions come true," Philip believes, "if only we can put our own house in order."

The second order of business for Philip is closely related to the first: the evangelization of the New World. "I believe there are millions of people in this country who are hungry for the bread of life and who thirst for the living water of Christ," Philip says. And his strategy is clear.

"First we must provide a parish home for our people who live in localities where there is no Orthodox Church. This is my first priority.

"Second, we must look at the building of pan-Orthodox parishes which worship in the language of the American people. This will help unite our people from various national origins.

"Third, and perhaps our greatest challenge, is to bring Christ to the people in this land who are not Christians and to those Christian people who seek the fullness of our apostolic faith."

The first two priorities, of course, have been in place for some time. But how does one go about mobilizing immigrants to reach out to the broad

American culture with a faith that is interpenetrated with the language, the music, the culture of ages past? Could Philip the bridge builder find a way to span the gap between the ethnic ghetto and mainstream America?

CHAPTER

14

New Friends

Those from among you
shall rebuild the old
waste places;
You shall raise up
the foundations of
many generations;
And you shall be called
the Repairer of the Breach,
the Restorer of the Streets
to Dwell In.

Isaiah 58:12

F or Metropolitan Philip, 1985 produced a twofold opportunity for dreams to come true. And the two events were interrelated.

THE VISIT OF PATRIARCH IGNATIUS IV

Patriarch Ignatius IV of Antioch was enthroned in 1979 after the death of Patriarch Elias. While both men were deeply spiritual and patriarchal in stature, there were marked differences in their manners. Elias was a charismatic man, spontaneous and prophetic when he preached. He was excitable, an enthusiast, with the ability to capture a congregation and move people to action.

By contrast, Ignatius, who studied philosophy at the American University of Beirut and theology at St. Sergius Institute in Paris, is the thinker, the keeper and defender of the Faith. He is pragmatic, methodical, not readily agitated. Above all, he is a man of great intellect and wisdom and is quietly and spiritually dynamic.

As Philip had done with Patriarch Elias in 1977, so he did with Patriarch Ignatius in 1985: he extended to him a specific invitation to come meet the faithful in America. The Patriarch accepted and arrived in New York in May 1985. In fluent English he acknowledged the welcome of those who met his plane, and his genuine warmth was wonderfully communicated.

The American press was especially taken with him because of his ecumenical activity. At home, he is president of the Middle East Council of Churches. Worldwide, he is known and respected by both protestant and Roman Catholic church leaders. Thus he was interviewed by countless reporters and given extensive television coverage everywhere he traveled.

In his travels in the Eastern United States, he was honored with an honorary doctorate at St. Vladimir's Orthodox Seminary in Crestwood, New York, and he presided over the dedication of the Heritage and Learning Center at Antiochian Village. He was received by numerous Orthodox hierarchs, including Archbishop Iakavos of the Greek Orthodox Church and Metropolitan Theodosius of the Orthodox Church in America.

Then came the trip West. The fact is that people from the Middle East have no concept of geographical distances in North America. You can travel from Damascus to Beirut, for example, in just over an hour. Thus, if the bishop of Zahle decides to journey to Beirut, it is for him a major trip, upwards of a forty-minute drive. And when he returns to Zahle, it may take him much of the week to rest up from the journey. Lebanon is about the size of Delaware.

When Philip and the Patriarch boarded the plane bound from New York to Los Angeles in early June, the metropolitan was lying in wait for the first hierarchical complaint. One hour passed, then two.

"Where is this Los Angeles?" the Patriarch asked.

"Be patient, Your Beatitude," Philip answered with an assuring smile.

"But we've been in the air over two hours," the Patriarch objected.

"Just wait a bit longer," said Philip. It took five and a half hours for them to reach the Los Angeles airport.

"How was that?" the metropolitan kidded when they landed.

"Lord have mercy," sighed the Patriarch. "This was an awful trip!" Why, it's farther than from London to Damascus."

"That is right," agreed the metropolitan. "And now do you understand why I want more bishops over here?"

The Patriarch nodded with a no-argument-you-have-made-your-point countenance. "Yes I do. I understand."

Philip made a mental note. Perhaps the time was approaching to begin thinking of a fourth bishop to share the load with Archbishop Michael, Bishop Antoun, and himself.

The West Coast clergy and laity had not yet met their father from Damascus, and they were impressed with his fluency in English and his remarkable ability to relate to his American flock.

THE EVANGELICALS

During the Patriarch's visit in Los Angeles, something unique happened in the life of the Orthodox Church in the New World. "Perhaps nothing like it has happened since the conversion of Russia," Philip remarked.

"We were at the Western parish life conference over the Memorial Day weekend when Father John Bartke, pastor of St. Michael's Church, Van Nuys, called to confirm that a delegation of three gentlemen would like to come and see His Beatitude and myself."

Father Bartke told the metropolitan, "They represent some two thousand evangelical protestant Christians who are interested in entering the Orthodox Church."

"Fine! Let me look at my schedule," Philip answered.

He checked the calendar and called Father John back the next day to set the appointment for the visit at eleven the morning of June 19, in the patriarchal suite at the Sheraton Universal hotel.

On the appointed day, three tall gentlemen walked in to see the visiting Orthodox hierarchs.

"I remember receiving them at the door," Philip said. "It was Peter Gillquist, Jon Braun, and Richard Ballew. They were three of the original leaders of the Evangelical Orthodox Church."

In the mid 1960s the group of people who formed the original core of leadership for this evangelical Christian movement served on the staff of Campus Crusade for Christ. Through a growing awareness of the grace of God, the need for revitalization of the contemporary Church, and the necessity for people to be born again into the Church instead of apart from it, they resigned their posts in Campus Crusade in 1968 and took beginning steps toward the building of Christian communities. Out of these initial efforts, a network of house churches was established in the early 1970s in an effort to follow carefully the teachings concerning the Church in the New Testament.

In concert with the building of new parishes, the group undertook a study of the Church in the early centuries of Christianity. Gradually, the movement became committed to the great and historic creeds of Christendom and adopted the episcopal form of government. Their worship became liturgical and sacramental in nature. A number of independent Christian pastors and their congregations joined in and became part of the fledgling body.

After nearly a decade of growth, the movement was formed into a definable structure in 1979, the Evangelical Orthodox Church. One of the few denominations in Church history not formed by a split from another church body, the EOC was instead a coming together of numerous independent communities across North America.

The new denomination attracted national attention and drew accolades from religious and secular commentators as well as severe criticism from a handful of evangelical opponents who expressed concern over the newfound Orthodoxy of the EOC.

"A new Christian denomination has been formed, combining some of the personal zeal of the evangelical movement and the traditional ritual of Eastern Orthodoxy, two forms of Christianity that do not easily overlap," announced the *New York Times,* in a copyrighted article by George Vecsey in early 1979. "The new group, the Evangelical Orthodox Church, is being formed by people with evangelical backgrounds who maintain that it is time for Christians to return to a structured church rather than experience God [just] as individuals."

Dr. Thomas Howard, writing in the *New Oxford Review,* July–August, 1979, observed, "Heaven itself knows what hilarious renewing would come to the poor old Catholic Church if one-half of her bishops took their pastoral and magisterial office one-half as seriously as these men in the Evangelical Orthodox Church."

Philip met and visited briefly at the door with the EOC leaders. Then they walked across the room for introductions to Patriarch Ignatius IV. The three visitors talked with the Orthodox hierarchs about their discovery of the ancient Christian faith and their quest to be incorporated into the fold of the Orthodox Church.

PATRIARCHAL RESPONSE

After about forty-five minutes of pleasant conversation, the Patriarch looked directly at Philip and said, "I want you to do anything you can to help them."

Philip in turn said to the evangelicals, "Please do two things. Send me a history of the Evangelical Orthodox Church starting at the beginning, including a profile of each parish, where it is, the number of members and a word about the pastor. Second, include with this information copies of the books and articles you have written. I will study your case carefully, and I will give you an answer soon."

Patriarch Ignatius remained in the United States through the days of the archdiocesan convention in Boston, Massachusetts. By Saturday night just before the closing convention banquet, the Patriarch was exhausted. He knew the program could go well beyond midnight. In contrast to Arabic banquet tradition, in which there is no preplanned program but only a time for very brief spontaneous speeches, Ignatius IV dreaded American banquets in which the speeches go on endlessly, out to the crack of doom.

The head table, some forty people in number, was lined up outside the banquet hall, ready to march in one by one for formal introductions. The Patriarch, last in line and standing next to Philip, was imposing in his black jibbe, with white-gray hair and beard and holding his long wooden staff.

A little boy of five or six walked up and stood directly in front of him, staring up into his face with reverential awe. "Where are you going?" the lad asked the Patriarch in a soft, breathy voice.

The tired Patriarch looked down at his admiring inquisitor and answered patiently, "To the Last Judgment!"

Philip and the entire back end of the line collapsed in laughter, gaining their composure just in time for the introductions.

In his memorable address to the banquet gathering, Philip appealed directly to his arch-shepherd for help in achieving Orthodox unity.

Your Beatitude, all the Orthodox in North America, regardless of national background, look up to you for guidance and leadership. They have been very encouraged by the

positive statements which you have made vis-
a-vis Orthodox unity on this continent. With
all my respect for all Orthodox Patriarchs, you
are the only Patriarch in the world today who
has enough freedom and courage to dialogue
sincerely and effectively with both the Greeks
and Slavs. Antioch, as you well stated, does
not have the "illusions of the first, second, or
third Rome."

Being fully cognizant of this reality, please
permit me to borrow an expression from the
president of our country and ask you, "If not
you, who? And if not now, when?"

The speech was interrupted by a standing
ovation, which lasted several minutes.

In mid August, Patriarch Ignatius IV prepared for his departure. "You have been a tremendous spiritual blessing to all of us," Philip assured
him as they said good-bye at the airport. "We are
grateful for your visit, and you have made many,
many new friends."

During the Patriarch's visit to America,
Philip received word from home that his father,
Elias Saliba, had departed this life at ninety-four
years of age. Philip's memories returned to that
bright Sunday morning when, as an impression-
able teenager, he obeyed his father's summons to
the monastery to meet the Patriarch. Then scenes
of Advents past and the after-work hours with his

father at their home shone in Philip's mind. "He was all a son could ever want, and more," Philip said. Another era had ended in his life.

As summer drew to a close, Philip returned to Englewood and to mounds of waiting correspondence. Besides this, there was planning and preparation for a busy autumn. By Labor Day, two large boxes of material arrived at his office from California. They contained the reports, articles, and books he had requested from the leaders of the Evangelical Orthodox Church. "To my surprise, I found that when I read their writings, they were not only Orthodox—but super Orthodox," Philip remarked.

Bishop Antoun walked into the metropolitan's office one afternoon as Philip was reading an issue of the EOC magazine, *Again*. "I don't understand why these people have been outside the Church for ten years, knocking on Orthodox doors," Philip told Antoun. "Here we say we believe the Lord's command, 'Go ye therefore and make disciples of all nations,' and these people who love the Orthodox Church, who believe in the Orthodox faith, haven't found a way to be received. I don't know of anyone who has studied St. Athanasius or Ignatius of Antioch more than they have. Look—read this article!"

Bishop Antoun began himself to do some reading. He had not yet met the EOC people.

"I cannot understand this: Why have we put them off?" Philip continued as he read further. "We

would rejoice if people from the Antiochian archdiocese wrote things like this and if all the reports
you and I get from activities with the Orthodox
Church were this positive."

Philip wrote back to Peter Gillquist, the presiding bishop of the EOC, to set a date for a meeting with him in March 1986. "I met with Father
Peter that next spring. We just sat down and talked
for the better part of the day. We laid down a number of points to guide our deliberations. And I remember telling him, 'If we can agree on these
points, then you're in!'"

Peter Gillquist brought the nine-point out-
line back and discussed it with the synod of the
Evangelical Orthodox Church at a meeting in
June, and then he contacted Metropolitan Philip
once again. "We would like all of us on the EOC
synod to come to Englewood and go over these
matters with you personally. Our men want very
much to meet you and talk face to face."

"When I heard that, I felt very, very happy,
very good about it," Philip recalls. "I really wanted
to meet everybody myself." His busy summer
schedule was already filled so a meeting date was
set in September 1986, at the archdiocesan headquarters.

In early September, about thirty people—
fifteen EOC clergy and fifteen observers—came to
meet with the metropolitan. He had asked Fathers
Joseph Allen and Paul Tarazi, Dr. John Boojamra,
and, of course, Bishop Antoun to take part. It was

a time of serious interaction as many probing questions were asked by both sides. And the tougher the questions, the more significant the answers were that followed. Everyone sensed that new ground was being cultivated. Never before had an evangelical protestant body asked to become part of the Orthodox Church. "I sat there quietly—listening and observing," Philip remembers.

The meeting grew in intensity and emotion as these men—and two thousand people with them—faced a monumental decision. After several hours one of the members of the EOC delegation, a former Southern Baptist pastor, Gordon Walker from Nashville, Tennessee, spoke up: "Your Eminence, brothers, we have been knocking on Orthodox doors for ten years. And today we have come to your doorstep. If you won't take us, then where do we go from here?" He broke down and cried.

"I will never forget that," the metropolitan told a meeting of Orthodox priests some days later. "That touched me so deeply. From that very moment, I had the sense that the decision to accept them was already made by God the Holy Spirit Himself, that everything would end up in the right place. We ended the meeting at the headquarters with prayer that day."

That was Friday afternoon. The next day, Saturday, the meeting moved to St. Anthony Church in nearby Bergenfield, New Jersey, where Philip observed the EOC liturgy.

On Monday morning the EOC delegation

would meet by themselves at St. Vladimir's Seminary, forty minutes away in the New York City suburb of Crestwood, to make a decision. The meeting on Monday at St. Vladimir's was not long. Within five minutes, the overwhelming consensus of the EOC was yes. "I remember Peter Gillquist calling me on the phone Monday afternoon asking to come and see me two days later on Wednesday," Philip says.

On Wednesday they came together, all thirty members of the EOC delegation, and broke the news to Metropolitan Philip that they had decided to join the Antiochian Orthodox Christian Archdiocese of North America. "I said to them from the depths of my heart, 'Welcome Home!'" Both groups agree it is home indeed.

"This is the brightest chapter in my entire ministry," Philip reflects. "With all the things that have happened in the archdiocese, to me this was the Orthodox Church in action. We have been a missionary movement from the very beginning. Jesus went from one place to another preaching and healing—He was the Missionary *par excellence*. And this is how He wants us to be today—a missionary Church, not a lazy, stagnant structure accepting the world as it is, taking on the status quo of the culture. No! He calls us to be transformers, to bring things back to God."

Philip Saliba is a radical and a risk taker. He believes that the indecisive will never change history, never redeem time. "If we are dead, if we don't respond to the Holy Spirit, then the Holy Spirit doesn't do anything," he tells his flock wherever he goes. "This is *synergia,* the basic biblical principle guiding our life in Christ, our working together with God. God issues the challenge, and we must respond. When I found myself faced with His challenge concerning the EOC, God said to me, 'Where are you? Do something about this.' And something was done."

The Evangelical Orthodox people were given a royal welcome home.

PENTECOST REVISITED

At first, Philip set the time for ordinations and chrismations of these new friends for a year away, summer or fall of 1987. "But I couldn't wait," he confessed. "I was so eager to go through with it, to bring them in by Easter. Theologically, they were set. If there is something lacking in the liturgical practice, I reasoned, we will take care of that as we grow together in the archdiocese!"

Ever the dreamer who decides, he moved the starting date to February 8, 1987, with the first chrismations and ordinations starting at St. Michael Church, Van Nuys, California. Ernest Saykaly flew into L.A. from Montreal for the occasion, and other archdiocesan priests and leaders came great distances as well.

"Truthfully, I have never, ever in my whole life had the spiritual experience that I did on that

Sunday," Philip said a short time later. "To receive
these people, to chrismate these beautiful little children, parents with their babes, receiving them into
the Orthodox Church . . . it was an incredible experience. Here we were, invoking the grace of God
on these people, receiving them into the bosom of
the Church born on Pentecost—the Church of the
New Testament—bringing them into full communion with that great cloud of witnesses throughout
almost two thousand years of Christian history.
What a great joy!"

From St. Michael's to the following Sunday
at St. Nicholas Cathedral in Los Angeles, and then
on to Sts. Peter and Paul near Santa Cruz, to Nashville and the South, to the Midwest, Canada,
Alaska, and the Pacific Northwest—seven central
areas in all—Metropolitan Philip, Bishop Antoun,
and Archdeacon Hans conducted the services of
anointing and ordination. "Every time I presided
over the Divine Liturgy or chrismated people from
the EOC and ordained priests and deacons, I felt
that the book of Acts was coming alive all over
again," Philip said.

Each step of the way, from each new parish,
Philip relayed the news by letter to Damascus, doing everything with the blessing of His Beatitude,
Ignatius, the Patriarch of Antioch. "Remember the
three gentlemen who came to visit you in California?" Philip asked him one Sunday afternoon by
long distance. "This is the movement; this is the
group. They have embraced the Orthodox faith,

and with your blessings and your prayers they will help bring America to Orthodox belief. You would be happy with me if you could be here."

On March 13, 1987, the Patriarch of Antioch responded with a personal letter to Philip and to his Church in America:

We have received your letter dated 2-24-87, which brought to us the good news that you have begun receiving the Evangelical brethren into the jurisdiction of the Holy See of Antioch. In the name of the Holy Synod of Antioch, we bless your glorious work in which we see an unique Antiochian initiative for which the Church is in dire need. This initiative destroys traditional, ethnic, national, and cultural barriers. Furthermore, it liberates the Orthodox Faith from the certain old formalism which froze, confined, victimized, and suffocated the universality of the Orthodox spirit; all that in the name of past history.

The Orthodox Church is not only for one nation, one civilization, and one continent; it is like God, Himself, for all and for every place. We reiterate our thankfulness and blessings for your great initiative, congratulating our new children, hoping that they will inspire us towards a stronger evangelism and a deeper comprehension of the Divine Word.

Along with the accolades, a few objections attended Philip Saliba's reception of the EOC. He was stubbornly rebuked by some Orthodox clerics because of his multiple ordinations of the EOC clergy. But he defended his action vigorously from the ancient practice of the Church in the New Testament and from the theological point of view of the early fathers. "Saidna won the war with his critics," says Joseph Allen. "He was never threatened by the use of canon law because he knows that the Canon of canons is the Holy Scripture. And that's exactly where he went."

He challenged his detractors to produce one single shred of evidence against multiple ordinations from the Bible or from the consensus of the Church. Granted, in its recent history the Orthodox custom had been to ordain one deacon and one priest at a service. But not so anciently, and not so in 1987. "Suppose in the future we would have a denomination with a thousand ministers—or ten thousand—want to join the Orthodox Church?" Philip asked. "How would you do it, one on one? Be serious! What on earth is wrong with multiple ordinations?"

He gave the ex-protestants a specific name: the Antiochian Evangelical Orthodox Mission. His purpose in doing so was to create a movement for evangelism within the archdiocese.

"*Antiochian* means that they belong to the Antiochian archdiocese. Second, they are *Orthodox*. Third, I want them always to remember that they are *Evangelical*. And last, they are a *Mission*. If they can't missionize and evangelize America, who can? They have studied the Bible very well and have studied Church history very well. Some of them are outstanding teachers. Now that they have come, their challenge is to bring America to Orthodoxy.

"Orthodoxy has been here for almost two hundred years—but it's still the best kept secret on the North American continent. I don't expect those who speak in foreign tongues to bring America to Orthodoxy because people don't understand Arabic, Russian, or Greek over here.

"Again I say, this is the brightest moment of my entire life from the beginning until now. I have invested so much hope in the AEOM as a movement."

ANOTHER FAREWELL

The joy of springtime 1987 was mingled with grief in September with the falling asleep of the Right Reverend Ellis Khouri in Grand Rapids, Michigan. He had encouraged Philip to be the leader of the Church in America from the time he had served as the priest at St. George Church in Cleveland.

Father Ellis was the dean of the Antiochian clergy in America, carrying the title of *protosyngelos,* the first in honor among the priests.

Philip traveled to Grand Rapids to officiate personally at the funeral and to say farewell to one of his dearest friends.

15

Dreaming Ahead: The Baptism of America

See, I have set before you
an open door, and no
one can shut it.

Revelation 3:8

P hilip Saliba has one leftover dream. He has dreamed it many times, and certainly progress has been made toward its realization. But the truth is, it isn't truly fulfilled yet. In Orthodox terminology, it would be called the Baptism of America.

In using this phrase he does not mean every man, woman, and child on the North American continent would become Orthodox. The phrase is meant to express the dream that Orthodox Christianity will be embraced broadly enough in the United States and Canada to interpenetrate the very life of the land.

Historically, nearly everywhere that the Orthodox Church has spread, it has visibly influenced the nation in which it has been planted and nourished. You cannot talk about Greece, for example, without talking Orthodox Christianity. It is the faith of the people. There is similarly no history of Russia apart from the history of the Russian Orthodox Church. The same can be said of countries like Romania, Bulgaria, Georgia, Syria, Lebanon, and Ethiopia.

An Orthodox America—what would it be like? If it happened, we would, to some degree at least, live in a Christian culture. There would be a new spirit in the land, much as in Ireland in the aftermath of St. Patrick, in Byzantium in the era of the seven ecumenical councils, in Russia in the centuries after St. Vladimir. At no time in her history has North America been Orthodox. The seeds of Orthodox Christianity have been planted, and the faith has certainly taken root. We know what Greek Orthodoxy is like in Greece, Russian Orthodoxy in Russia, but we are not yet clear on what American Orthodoxy would be like because there is, as of yet, very little Orthodoxy here that is indigenously, genuinely, visibly American. The reason most Orthodox Christianity on this continent still looks so ethnic is because it is.

What would it be like to live in a nation here in the West where a significant part of the population—leaders and citizens—were part of a Christianity that prioritized worship of God the Father, Son, and Holy Spirit above all else? Can we imagine a Church with a sacramental worldview, not that some things are secular, some sacred, but that all of life is to be lived as an offering to the Lord? Could there be a body of people who not only receive the faith of the apostles as revealed in the New Testament and live it out in the Christian tradition in the Church, but who are committed to preserve that faith and not negotiate its change or compromise? Is it possible for people to live godly and righteous lives, without judging others or forcing their faith on those who choose not to obey it? The thought is mind stretching, is it not?

What is holding the Orthodox Church back? There are, after all, six or seven million adherents in North America! Besides the fact that nobody makes the claim that all these millions are hard-core disciples of the faith, another huge factor militates against the reality of the Baptism of America: ethnic division.

In Greece, there is one Orthodox Church under one primate. In Russia there is one Church under one primate. In America, depending on how you count primates, there are either fourteen or fifteen. These Orthodox bodies all share the same polity, celebrate the same liturgy, believe the same doctrine, and even commune with each other. But administratively they are under separate authorities. They function, for the most part, independently of each other.

Philip's dream is for one primate, one Orthodox Church of America, and for a number of good reasons. The first is for the glory of God. The second is, it is utterly noncanonical—it is heresy—to have multiple jurisdictions in one nation. And third, until the Orthodox Church is unified, she cannot be effectively mobilized to transform North America.

The dream of the Baptism of America cannot be realized until the dream for unity of the Orthodox Church in North America comes true.

Philip Saliba believes the dream is not only do-able, it is inevitable. But stemming the progress is the human tendency to hold onto turf—in this case, ethnic turf. It is not a matter of pointing fingers, he believes. Everyone has participated in feeding the problem. His dream is that everyone will participate in finding the solution.

THE DREAM UNVEILED

Those who have followed closely the ministry of Metropolitan Philip over the twenty-five years he has been Archbishop remember back to 1984 and his speech on the Sunday of Orthodoxy in Worcester, Massachusetts. For in this address— probably the most prophetic of his twenty-five years as metropolitan—he unveiled his dream for all to hear. He called his message "Orthodoxy in America—Success and Failure":

Once every year, on the Sunday of Orthodoxy, the Orthodox people in America emerge from their ethnic islands to celebrate the triumph of the Orthodox Faith over the iconoclastic heresy. This victory happened in the year A.D. 787, one thousand, one hundred ninety-seven years ago. I am proud of our history; for those who have no past, have no

present and will have no future. There is a difference, however, between contemplating history and worshiping history.

During the first one thousand years of her
existence, the Church was courageous enough
to respond to the challenges of her time. Many
local councils were called, and seven ecumenical councils were convened to deal with important issues which the Church had to face.
The question now is: What happened to that
dynamism which characterized the life of the
Church between Pentecost and the tenth century?

Did God stop speaking to the Church?
Did the action of the Holy Spirit in the Church
cease after the tenth century? Why are we
always celebrating the remote past? Have we
been lost in our long, long history? I wish we
could gather to celebrate an event which happened five hundred years ago or two hundred
years ago or perhaps something which happened last year.

In the Gospel of St. John, our Lord said:
"My Father has been working until now, and I
have been working" (John 5:17). Thus, we
cannot blame God or the Holy Spirit for our
inaction. History, from a Christian perspective, is a dynamic process because it is the
arena of God's action in the past as well as in
the present. But, if we do not fully, creatively,
and faithfully respond to the divine challenge,

no change can be effected in our Church, values, and human situation. Our forefathers, motivated by the power of the Holy Spirit, have fought valiantly and triumphantly against iconoclasm and all kinds of heresies; *but the triumphs of the past will not save us from the sterility of the present and the uncertainty of the future.*

It is indeed astonishing that we have not had an ecumenical council since A.D. 787 despite the many changes which the Church has encountered during the past one thousand, one hundred ninety-seven years. I shall mention but a few of these global events which affected the life of the Church directly or indirectly since the last Ecumenical Council:

The 1054 schism between East and West
The fall of Constantinople
The European Renaissance with all its
    implications
The protestant Reformation
The discovery of the New World
The French Revolution
The Industrial Revolution
The Communist Revolution and its impact
    on the Orthodox Church
The First and Second World Wars
The dawning of the nuclear age
The exploration of space and all the
    scientific and technological discoveries
    which baffle the mind

Despite all these significant events which have deeply touched our lives, we Orthodox are still debating whether or not we should convene the Eighth Ecumenical Council.

A few days ago, I was glancing through the 1932 Arabic issue of the *Word* Magazine and came across the following news item, entitled "Pan Orthodox Consultations for an Ecumenical Council Were Postponed."

The news item continues: "The Orthodox world was expecting that the representatives of the Orthodox Churches would meet on Mount Athos during the Pentecost Season in June of this year for serious preparation for the Great Ecumenical Council. There was great concern as to what the Pan Orthodox consultations would decide regarding important and urgent issues facing the Church. What a disappointment to have learned that the meeting was postponed to the forthcoming year."

That meeting never took place, and I doubt if an ecumenical council will be convened in the foreseeable future.

You might ask, what is the reason behind this Orthodox stagnation? Did our history freeze after A.D. 787? There is no doubt that the rise of Islam, the collapse of the Byzantine Empire, and the fall of Tsarist Russia have contributed much to our past and present stagnation. The sad condition of our mother churches across the ocean is indicative of this reality.

The Patriarchate of Jerusalem is living under the heel of a Zionist state. The Coptic Orthodox patriarch of Egypt is still living under house arrest. And what can I say about Antioch? If I may paraphrase the biblical words, I would say the following: "A voice was heard in Lebanon, wailing and lamentation—Antioch weeping for her children; she refused to be consoled because they were no more" (Matt. 2:18).

The Church of Cyprus is suffering the consequences of a badly and sadly divided island. The ecumenical patriarchate is slowly, but surely, dying from Turkish oppression. Furthermore, the Patriarchate of Moscow and those of Eastern Europe continue to suffer under the yoke of communism.

Have we then lost all hope for an Orthodox renaissance? Is there not a place on this planet where we can dream of a better Orthodox future? I believe that there is a place, and this place is the North American continent. We have a tremendous opportunity in this land to dream dreams and see visions, only if we can put our house in order. Where in the whole world, today, can you find seven million free Orthodox except in North America?

We are no longer a Church of immigrants; the first Orthodox liturgy was celebrated in this country before the American Revolution. Many of our Orthodox young people have died on the battlefields of various wars, defending American ideals and principles. We have contributed much to the success of this country in the fields of medicine, science, technology, government, education, art, entertainment, and business.

We consider ourselves Americans and we are proud of it—except when we go to Church, we suddenly become Greeks, Russians, Arabs, and Albanians. Despite our rootedness in the American soil, our Church in America is still divided into fifteen jurisdictions, contrary to our Orthodox ecclesiology and canon law which forbid the multiplicity of jurisdictions in the same territory.

Individually, Orthodox jurisdictions have done much for themselves. We have some of the finest theological institutions in the world. We have excellent religious publications. Many volumes have been written in English on Orthodox theology. We have some of the best Christian education programs. Our clergy are highly educated and deeply committed to the Orthodox faith. We have built multimillion dollar churches and cathedrals, and our laity are well organized and have contributed generously to the financial and spiritual well-being of our parishes.

Collectively, however, we have not been able to rise above our ethnicity and work together with one mind and one accord for the glory of Orthodoxy. Our efforts continue to be scattered in different directions.

Why should we have fifteen departments for Christian education, media relations, sacred music, youth ministry, and clergy pensions? Where is our spiritual and moral impact on the life of this nation? Where is our voice in the media? Why is it that every time there is a moral issue to be discussed, a protestant, a Roman Catholic, and a Jew are invited for such discussions? How can we explain our Orthodox absence despite the authenticity of our theology and moral teachings?

The answer to these disturbing questions is simple: It is ethnicism. Unfortunately, we have permitted ourselves to become victims of our ethnic mentalities. We cannot be agents of change in full obedience to the truth unless we transcend ethnicism and establish a new Orthodox reality in North America.

I am not asking you to deny your own history and your own culture. What I am asking is to blend your old and new cultures into some kind of an integrated reality. I am not against ethnicism, if ethnicism means a return to the spirit of the desert fathers, the Syrian fathers, the Greek fathers, and the Slavic fathers. But if ethnicism means a narrow, fanatic ghetto mentality which separates us from each other, then I am definitely against such ethnicism.

The mission of the Church is not to be subservient to any kind of nationalism. The mission of the Church is the salvation of souls—all souls. In his epistle to the Galatians, St. Paul said: "There is neither Jew nor Greek, there is neither slave nor free, there is neither male nor female; for you are all one in Christ Jesus" (Gal. 3:28).

Brothers and sisters in Orthodoxy, I have shared with you, today, some of my reflections on our past and present, success and failure. I would like to share with you, now, some daring visions about the future.

My first vision concerns the role for our Orthodox laity in this relentless quest for Orthodox unity. After eighteen years in the episcopate, I have been convinced that Orthodox unity in America must begin on the grass roots level. You, the laity, are the conscience of the Church and the defenders of the faith. Consequently, I would like to see a strong pan-Orthodox lay movement, totally dedicated to the cause of Orthodox unity. Without the laity, our churches would be empty, and our liturgical and sacramental services would be in vain. The clergy and laity, working together, are the people of God, and they constitute the Orthodox Church.

My second vision concerns the Standing Conference of Orthodox Bishops in America (SCOBA). Since the purpose of SCOBA is to bring organic unity to our churches in America, I believe that SCOBA should be elevated to the rank of an Orthodox synod which will have the power to deal effectively and decisively with our Orthodox problems in this country.

My third vision, ladies and gentlemen, concerns the ecumenical patriarchate. There is no doubt that we need a catalyst to lead us from the wilderness of division to the promised land of unity and fulfillment. I do not know of a better catalyst than the ecumenical patriarch himself, who continues to live like a prisoner in Istanbul. Let us prevail on him to leave Turkey, come to America, and unite our various jurisdictions. The Greek remnant in Istanbul can be shepherded by an exarch, who would represent the ecumenical throne. The ecumenical patriarch will preserve his traditional role in the world regardless of where he resides.

We have unlimited opportunities in this free land, but if we do not move forward with faith and courage, our Church on this continent will remain an insignificant dot on the margin of history.

Finally, I would like to conclude this sermon with the words of the late Alexander Schmemann. "One can almost visualize the glorious and blessed day when forty Orthodox bishops of America will open their first synod in New York or Chicago or Pittsburgh with the hymn, 'Today the grace of the Holy Spirit assembled us together,' and will appear to us not as 'representatives' of Greek, Russian, or any other 'jurisdictions' and interests but as the very icon, the very 'Epiphany' of our unity within the body of Christ; when each of them and all together will think and deliberate only in terms of the whole, putting aside all particular and national problems, real and important as they may be. On that day, we shall 'taste and see' the oneness of the Orthodox Church in America."

AFTER HOURS

Each evening, when the work of the day is over, when the metropolitan is alone at home—perhaps Bishop Antoun and Archdeacon Hans are there with him—he climbs the stairs, goes to his quarters, slips on a pair of corduroy trousers and a cotton shirt, and gets comfortable.

He comes back downstairs after the network news is over, enjoys a low-cholesterol dinner, and retires to his chair in the living room.

He begins to dream.

Ask the priests in the archdiocese and they will say that this is their favorite time in all the world to be with the Boss. Because he dreams out loud.

Much of that time is spent in trying to determine how to build better bridges—to the other Orthodox jurisdictions, to those of his flock who are indifferent toward God and the Church, to other Christians he suspects would like to become Orthodox in their faith, to nonbelievers in need of the saving grace of Jesus Christ.

"When I was going to school in England," he mused one night in his easy chair, "our philosophy professor walked into the class and said, 'There are three main tragedies in life.'

"All present looked at him eagerly, curious to know what these three tragedies were.

"'These tragedies,' the professor said, 'are first, the tragedy of knowledge, for people who know a lot suffer greatly. The second tragedy is ignorance. And the third is the tragedy of dissatisfaction.'

"I find myself many times caught in this last tragedy. Regardless of how much is accomplished, I have a sense of dissatisfaction that still more can be done. So much has been done in the archdiocese in the last twenty-five years. But I am still dissatisfied. I think we could have done more."

The dream for Orthodox unity and for an Orthodox America keeps getting in the way of his satisfaction. He knows it. Everyone around him knows it.

"Whatever I have done for the Church in the past twenty-five years, I consider it to have been my duty. I consider it a gift from God that He gave me whatever wisdom, whatever vision, and whatever strength I have had to achieve the progress we have made in this beloved archdiocese.

"There is a passage in the New Testament which says that if you do what you are asked to do by the Lord, you say nothing except 'I am an unprofitable servant.' I have tried to do what the Lord commanded me to do. And yet despite all that, I continue to be restless. I continue to be dissatisfied."

Does this mean he is fraught with regrets? People will ask him, "If you had a chance to relive your life, would you live it differently?"

He tells them, "No. I would do exactly what I have done."

Or they ask him if he is depressed over the fact that the unity he has sought has thus far eluded him. "I would be, were it not that our unity as Orthodox into one American jurisdiction is inevitable. History is clear on that, and certainly the Scriptures are clear. Therefore we will simply continue our work for unity until our shameful division is overcome.

"Remember, history is a dynamic process. It does not stand still. There is nothing worse than stagnation, and it is the life-giving Holy Spirit who keeps us as a Church from ever throwing up our hands in despair."

The years have been good to Philip, and he has gained great favor with both God and man.

"I hope God gives me many more productive years," he admits. "But you know, when we are young, we go to bed dreaming of the sunrise. I believe I have reached a point in my life where I wake up in the morning and I start looking for the sunset."

His commitment to the faithful in the archdiocese is unwavering. He is there to serve. But there still awaits him, to his discomfort and consternation, the fulfillment of that all-important one last dream.

As he gathered his flock around him at the fortieth convention of the archdiocese in July 1991 in Washington, D.C., he made them a promise.

"Twenty-five years ago, on the top of a Lebanese mountain, which overlooks the deep valley where I was born, I made a vow. I would like to renew it today before God and before you, my beloved flock.

I promise to visit and watch over the flock now entrusted to me, after the manner of the apostles, whether they remain true to the faith and in the exercise of good works, more especially the priests; and to inspect with diligence, that there may be no schisms, superstitions, and impious veneration and that no customs contrary to Christian piety may injure Christian conduct.

And may God, who sees the heart, be the witness of my vow.

And may our Savior, Himself, be my helper, in my sincere zealous government and performance thereof. And unto Him, together with the Father and the Holy Spirit, be glory, dominion, honor, and worship, now and ever and unto all ages.

Amen."